Death and Deprivation on the Forgotten Sumatra Railway

Death and Deprivation on the Forgotten Sumatra Railway

A Prisoner's Story

James H. Banton

Pen & Sword
MILITARY

First published in Great Britain in 2021 by
Pen & Sword Military
An imprint of
Pen & Sword Books Ltd
Yorkshire – Philadelphia

ISBN 978 1 39900 649 1

A CIP catalogue record for this book is
available from the British Library.

Printed and bound in the UK by CPI Group (UK) Ltd, Croydon, CRO 4YY

Pen & Sword Books Limited incorporates the imprints of Atlas, Archaeology,
Aviation, Discovery, Family History, Fiction, History, Maritime, Military, Military
Classics, Politics, Select, Transport, True Crime, Air World, Frontline Publishing,
Leo Cooper, Remember When, Seaforth Publishing, The Praetorian Press,
Wharncliffe Local History, Wharncliffe Transport, Wharncliffe True Crime and
White Owl.

For a complete list of Pen & Sword titles please contact

PEN & SWORD BOOKS LIMITED
47 Church Street, Barnsley, South Yorkshire, S70 2AS, England
E-mail: enquiries@pen-and-sword.co.uk
Website: www.pen-and-sword.co.uk

Or
PEN AND SWORD BOOKS
1950 Lawrence Rd, Havertown, PA 19083, USA
E-mail: Uspen-and-sword@casematepublishers.com
Website: www.penandswordbooks.com

Contents

Preface

It is 1988. I am in my 69th year and my wife Dorothy is in her 67th year. At the request and prompting of Keith, the youngest of our four children, I, with Dorothy's help, will attempt to compile as correctly and honestly as I can the events of our lifetime.

This will not be a chronological diary, as I will add to each chapter as and when memories return to either of us.

It will be the story of two teenagers who met entirely by chance, fell immediately in love and have shared the highs and lows of life of ordinary people. Having both in completely different circumstances survived when the odds were stacked against us, we are in the autumn of our lives, still in love and enjoying what we recognize as our 'bonus years'.

Chapter 1

Early Days

I was born at No. 11 Victoria Street, Burton-on-Trent, Staffordshire, at 11.50am on Sunday, 6 June 1920 – a timing which my father thought was perfect as he was able to go along to his 'local' (The Lord Napier), which was then at No. 14 Victoria Street, to celebrate when they opened at noon on Sundays.

My father was one Ebenezer Banton and my mother was, prior to marriage, Elsie May Key.

I only knew one of my grandparents, on my mother's side, who was in her second marriage and was Elizabeth Chambers.

My mother had three brothers: Bill, Syd and Albert. Their father died when they were small children after suffering for some years as a result of an accident involving some Bass horses outside the Midland Hotel in Station Street. This had a large effect on my youth, as you will read later.

Bill gave a false age during the First World War and was driving lorries in France before he was 17 years old. He married Elsie Fitzjohn and they had one son, Bill, who when aged about 23 walked out of his widowed mother's house one day and was never heard of again.

Syd Key spent his whole life on the railway and moved to Normanton, Yorkshire, to advance from fireman to driver. He had two sons, Sydney and Peter, and lived to be about 70 years of age, leaving his wife Eadie (formerly Robinson) who died in 1984 at about 80 years of age.

Albert, the youngest (who introduced me to football), worked in the breweries until his death in his early 1960s. His widow Ethel (née Pratt from Bond Street) still lives in Branstone Road and has two sons, Bill and Brian, and two daughters, Eileen and Christine.

I never learned anything of my father's parents, and the reason for this was only recently made clear to me by my cousin, Richard Banton. It was the custom at that time (the turn of the twentieth century) that when children became 13 or 14 years of age they were forced to fend for themselves. This being the case, boys went mainly to farm service and girls into domestic service, and thus families disintegrated. Travel was scarce and the majority of parents could barely read or write adequately, so contacts were lost.

My father often told me how at the 'Statutes Fair', farmers from the outlying districts would come to 'hire hands'. They would meet youths wanting work and would hire them at about £20 per year plus keep (such as it was), and the deal was sealed by the payment to the 'hand' of one shilling (5p).

The young men (as did the girls in domestic service) would equip themselves with a large metal trunk, secured by a padlock, in which they would keep all their worldly belongings. Two of these (my mother's and my father's) were at our home and used as blanket chests. One was disposed of with rubbish when Kathleen left the Swan Hotel as landlady in the 1970s.

My father had two brothers of whom I knew, Samuel Henry and Frederick. Frederick, who lost an arm in the First Word War, worked as a railway guard. He died of cancer in Nottingham, leaving his wife Emmie with three small children: Jackie, Norman and Dennis. The last I knew of these (in about 1960), they were living in Oxford; Jack and Norman were working at Morris Motors and Dennis was the cricket coach to the University and playing in Minor Counties cricket.

Samuel Henry and his wife Elsie (née Jones, from Short Street, Stapenhill) had three sons – Raymond, Cecil and Richard – and one daughter, Edna.

Uncle Sam only had one eye, and on six days a week would leave the Co-op bakery in Byrkerley Street with his horse and van to deliver bread and cakes around Stanton, Newhall and district in all weathers. He retired after suffering an injury to a leg, and with his compensation became landlord of The Lord of Napier in Victoria Street. Cecil died in 1985, and Ray (Isle of Man), Richard (Wales) and Edna (Shropshire) have all left the home town.

My father went off into farm service somewhere in the district of Tunstall and Rangemore, while my mother (they had still not met at this stage) went into domestic service.

My mother went first to work at a boys' school at Rocester and later was house assistant at Denstone College near Uttoxeter. I remember Mother telling me how at 15 and 16 years old she would have to work from 5am until 10 or 11pm. The boys would come in after playing 'rugger', and as well as other chores she would be required to wash, dry and iron all their kit ready for the next day – no washing machines in those days; only human ones!

When she was a little older, Mother became a cook and later worked for Michael Sadler, a very highly respected vet who had his house and stables in Lichfield Street. The house still stands near the corner of Bond Street, opposite the entrance to Peel Croft.

In 1912, Father began work in the cooperage department of Samuel Allsopps brewery, which later became Ind Coope Allsopp and is now Allied Breweries. It was about this time that a friend of his by the name of Ian Mansfield (whose cobblers shop still operates in High Street opposite the Bass Brewery offices) introduced him to my mother.

The war broke out in 1914, and Ian and my father volunteered together almost immediately and were marched from the Drill Hall in Horninglow Street to the barracks at Lichfield.

Father, having become accustomed to horses, served as lead-driver with teams of six horses – or sometimes mules – in the Royal Field Artillery. He was trained in Ireland and saw service in the fiasco at the Dardanelles, as well as in Mesopotamia and India. He was on his way home from India at the end of the war when he learned that his father had died (in those days it was a journey of weeks by troopship).

Upon arriving home, it was not long before he and my mother were married. As mother was still with the Sadlers, it was Mrs Sadler who provided the wedding cake and provisions for the reception as an appreciation of her loyal service. Such acts were not often shown to 'staff', and I understand was well talked about at the time. The wedding took place at All Saints' Church on Branston Road.

Mother and Dad settled at No. 11 Victoria Street, and here I am not absolutely certain what the situation was – but when I was a child there was a saying 'Little pigs have big ears', which meant young children heard things which they were not intended to hear.

From these overheard conversations, I learned that there was an old lady who was always referred to as the 'Old Dutch'. I have a feeling that this could have been my grandmother Banton (which I doubt) or an aunt who with age had become senile. In those days, senility was something regarded as shameful and was not talked about. What is certain is that whoever it was did not live long, or was probably even dead before my parents went to live there. There was certainly a long sofa there belonging to her which would easily seat five people. My mother would cover it with pretty fabrics which she would wash and iron, and it was still in use long after the second war. Whoever the old lady was, she was certainly not there when I was born in 1920.

My memories of pre-school days of course are few, but I do recall people in the front room of our house. I have vague recollections of seeing in there a high shop-counter construction and of someone occasionally being taken ill. In later years I learned that a tailor and tailoress hired this room as a workshop. As a result, I was the best-dressed kid in the district. It was later explained to me that the lady in question was prone to fits.

I can remember my Uncle Syd living with us, and the smell of ammonia as he constantly pressed and cleaned his suits. There was no Sketchleys cleaners in Burton in those days. Uncle Syd was always, even in old age, immaculate in his appearance, and was renowned for this, even in his overalls on the footplate and for the condition of his highly polished black metal box with its brass fasteners which footplatemen carried their food in.

After Syd married and left us, Bill came to take his place, but this had its problems. Bill was a talented man who could do any manner of jobs – even cobbling shoes. He was an exceptionally good artist, in colour or black and white. Unfortunately, being a very heavy smoker led to his death in his early 50s. Beer also caused him many problems, and working at Bass he was, to say the least, often very 'anti-social' when he came home in the evenings.

My father liked a drink too, but with him that extra one had the opposite effect; always a happy character, he became even more so and would give his soul away at such times. The contrast often caused friction, and on the most volatile occasion the pair came to fighting. As a result, Mother, Dad and I went to Uncle Sam's house in Henry Street (off Casey Lane and now demolished) and slept the night on the floor.

Upon returning home on the Sunday, we found that Bill had taken a saucepan of boiling water upstairs to throw on anyone who approached him, but had fallen. He was badly scalded around his head, and I remember him wearing the bandages for a long time. Drink often got him into trouble at work, but he always kept his job, even when thousands were out of work and the sack was easy to come by, such was his talent.

Living at No. 10 were Mr and Mrs Corton and their daughter Beatrice. Mr Corton – always referred to by his wife as 'the master' – worked for LMS Railway labelling loads of ale from the nearby Freeman's brewery (now East Staffordshire Borough Council) site in Derby Street. He was a big man, with not a hair on his head, was bow-legged – exaggerated by wearing knee-length leather leggings – and was nicknamed 'Moses' by my mother. His wife Betty was a small tyrant of a woman who was moon-struck and very hostile. She had a fixation that her husband had a 'fancy woman' (what an imagination!). She would work herself up into a frenzy, and a regular antic was to wash the axe in the water butt and proclaim, 'I'll murder the old bugger when he comes home but it will be a clean cut' – she never did. At these times we would all stay indoors so as not to provoke her – and for safety's sake. Often on Saturday nights, when 'the master' returned from his local, she would smash the window in her outbursts, and on occasions the odd one of ours too. Poor 'Moses' would spend Sunday replacing them. Sometimes the police intervened and would call on my parents for statements, but I don't think they wished to get implicated too much.

At No. 12 lived a grand 'olde worlde' couple, typical of old England pictures, who were known to us all as Gran and Grandad Fitzjohn.

Gran was shaped like a barrel, had her white hair parted down the middle and into a bun at the back, and was always dressed in black – even her apron. When she made her way to the corner shop or The Benbow (the opposite corner to Timboard timber merchants in Princess Street), she always wore her bonnet. Times were hard, but Gran would share whatever she had, even her half-pint as she carried it back in a bottle. Women didn't drink in pubs in those days, so Gran visited the 'outdoor'.

Grandad was short and stout, with white hair and a full white beard and moustache. He always wore a gold watch chain and Albert across his waistcoat. Both of them deservedly lived into their 80s. Grandad never had to wear spectacles, and into his last days he would sit in the Napier and score for the darts players, from the far side of the room.

With them lived a daughter, Florrie (still living there in her mid-80s), and a lodger – they married and became Mr and Mrs Meadows.

At No. 13 lived Charlie Fitzjohn (son from No. 12) and his wife Ada. I can't remember Charlie ever working due to his ill health, but he passed his time pegging rugs from old clothes torn into strips and he would clean and paint up the old-fashioned mangles, all to make a few coppers. On his less-well days he would pass his time doing jigsaw puzzles. Ada was the local information bureau and was renowned for her sayings, some of which were not very lady-like, but many of which I remember. They had a family of daughters: Elsie married Uncle Bill; Lily became Mrs Aingar (Eddie's mother); while Doris and Mary still live at No. 13.

These four houses shared a common 'entry' – two properties on either side – and so we lived.

Chapter 2

School Days

I well remember my first day at school. I entered through what seemed to me a large iron gate with huge pillars on either side, turned left and through a huge door into Victoria Road Infants' School. This, although one part of a three-school building of that name, was, and still is, in York Street. Next to it is what was then the girls' school, and in Victoria Road was the boys' school. Each was complete with its own yard, with an open-sided shed in which hung a large black box for litter known as the 'Tidy box'.

During play-time, some mothers would come to the railings with sandwiches for their offspring, whom they would leave crying as they left.

The headmaster of these schools was one C.J. ('Keggy') Cumber (father of a Renold Chains draughtsman), and he became a personality of my school life. Keggy was a huge man in height, in girth and in character, and was very strict but very fair.

Annual sports day was held at Peel Croft, where all the schools would compete as teams and as individuals. The proceedings would start at 10am and would go on until 8pm, with heats and finals of every kind from 100-yard sprints to relays, netball, tug of war, etc. Controlling all this was Keggy Cumber, who stood all day in the middle of the field dressed in white suit and panama hat, using a megaphone (no amplifiers or loud hailers in those days). He must have lost a few stones on each occasion, and I can still see him as he ploughed his way through the programme without losing his sense of humour, only taking time out to mop his brow. It took some fellow to do this, and Keggy was some fellow, liked, feared and respected by every kid in Burton.

On some national occasion, I think a royal visit, he trained a massed-choir of hundreds of school kids from all over town. One of the things they sang was 'We'll keep a welcome in the hillsides', so I suppose it was the visit of the Prince of Wales, who later abdicated as King.

I later moved on to the boys' school in Victoria Road, and what is now a narrow strip of asphalt was a garden where we learned our nature studies. In the two years of my stay here, I can only recall one occasion when we marched to the Outwoods Recreation Ground to have races and play games. I enjoyed this school and made a name for myself in the art class, and for my efforts Keggy signed my book of pastels and wrote in the cover, 'Well done Jim' (this book is still about somewhere). I was also given a book and a box of pastels, which meant I had two Christmases that year.

One thing which I particularly recall from these days was the first Burton bus service, which ran along Victoria Road, Waterloo Street and through town to Anglesey Road via Branston Road as 'Route 5'. It returned via Uxbridge Street, the town centre and Victoria Road to Derby Road as 'Route 6'.

The coming of buses was a godsend to people who previously had to walk long distances to a tramway service which only ran along principal streets: Horninglow Road, Victoria Crescent, Waterloo Street to Station Street, then from Station Street via High Street and Branston Road to the Leicester line bridge or via High Street and Trent Bridge to the Swan Hotel, thence to either Winshill or Stapenhill.

I also remember a much-disliked teacher called Paddy Hogan. With spectacles on the end of his nose, trilby on the back of his head and clips on his trouser bottoms, he would stretch himself over his bike to mount from a scooting start over the rear wheel from the back-step. The back-step was an extension to the rear axle, and passengers would stand on this, kneeling on the carrier and holding the rider's shoulder. This is not allowed now of course. It was always a mystery as to why Paddy Hogan's bike had more flat tyres than anyone else's, but that was a mystery everyone knew the answer to!

It was whilst I was at this school that Dr Frewer came to the house one evening and sent my sisters Winifred and Margaret to the Isolation Hospital with diphtheria. Winifred became so ill that my parents had to go dressed in white caps and gowns into the ward to visit her. The usual practice was to stand outside and look through the window. For over two years, my two sisters and myself were, in turn, patients with either diphtheria or scarlet fever.

The Isolation Hospital was situated where the Geoffrey Hodges wing now stands, and the main entrance off Belvoir Road is still the same today. It consisted of three blocks: a Fever Block, Diphtheria Block and Sanatorium. The 'San' was for tuberculosis patients, and the only treatment for that was fresh air and isolation. All these diseases, which were rife in my childhood, have now been eliminated by vaccines.

Upon contracting one of these diseases, Mr Hopkins, who lived in the lodge house by the main gate, would bring a big brown wooden van and take you to hospital. The next day, men would come to the house and seal all the doors and windows whilst it was fumigated by the burning of chemicals. Afterwards, the smell hung around for days.

The Sister in charge of this hospital was Sister Perry, who would appear in my life later on.

During this two-year period, my sister Kathleen was born. I recall her lying in the coach-work of an old pram used as a crib. When only a baby, she had an abscess on her neck and mother would not allow the doctor to lance it because of the scar which would be left, preferring to treat it herself until it was cleaned and healed. I had a further sister who was born with spina bifida and who only lived for ten days.

At some time during my four years at Victoria School, I went to visit my Uncle Syd and Aunty Eadie at Normanton in Yorkshire. While there, I slipped when climbing a low wall to visit a playmate, which resulted in me sustaining a hernia. The doctor came, made me comfortable and confined me to a bed, but on the following day my pal from next door came to stay with me whilst my aunt nipped out to the shops. Boys being boys, we ventured out into the street and I got knocked over by a motorcycle, and thus ended the holiday!

Sometime later and back at home, the hernia gave acute pain late one Saturday evening and the ambulance took me to Burton Infirmary. The ambulance was an ex-army vehicle with canvas sides held together with straps, and my father and Uncle Bill were guessing by turns which route we were taking to New Street.

I woke the following morning (Sunday) in a ward of about thirty beds, all covered with scarlet blankets. At the far end of the ward, a group of children were sat around a large coal fire, making toast for all our breakfasts.

Later in my stay, I looked through a window into what I now know was Duke Street, trying to catch a sight of the Statutes Fair. To my surprise, there stood my Dad and Uncle Bill with a huge teddy bear. I later learned that they had spent their last 2d (old money) to win this for me.

Operations in those days were performed by one's own GP, and mine was done by Dr Pickering-Lowe of Bridge Street surgery, who upon visiting me at home later, found me playing in the street. Without further ado, he picked me up, put me under his arms and took me indoors.

I was also at home with measles around this time, and on a hot summer day was sat in the back yard drawing when the school-board man came.

I was alone and my mother was at No. 12 assisting, as people did at such times, at the birth of Ted Meadows. The school-board man, 'Knocker Johnson', struck terror in all the kids. He always dressed in black, from his bowler hat to his shiny boots, and always carried an umbrella under his arm as he shuffled his way round and checked up on every half-day off from school.

When a reorganisation of schooling took place, those from 9 to 11 years old were moved to Grange Street. These two years were spent preparing for the dreaded 'Eleven Plus' exam, with the prize of a place at Central or Grammar School.

Looking back, this was a fairly uneventful two years, apart from the sweat to try to pass the exam. The first headmaster was Freddie Waring – tall, white-haired and bespectacled. Upon the retirement of Freddie he was replaced by 'Bowie' Templeman – short, with black hair around a bald pate, a black moustache and bow-legged. Bowie had been a junior teacher at Stafford Street School in the days when my father was one of his pupils.

One of the teachers was Eddie Hardwick, one of the jeweller sons; he played for Burton Rugby Club, who at this time were a force to be reckoned with. Eddie ran a team from Grange Street, in which I played only twice. On one occasion we played Christ Church, and one lad in their team stuck in my mind – he was as hard as nails, always laughing, and had a mop of blond hair. I was to meet up with him later.

While at Grange Street, we were all called out onto the playground to watch the *R100* airship fly slowly over. This was the largest airship ever built, and was symbolic for me because it was built at and operated from Cardington in Bedfordshire, where some years later I was to become a member of the RAF. A sister ship to this was built, the *R101*, which crashed in France with the loss of all on board. Thus the airship project was halted and *R100* was scrapped. The specially built hangers were used during the war to build barrage balloons.

Eventually came the days of the 'Eleven Plus', and then the long wait for the result. It was to be announced at the assembly tomorrow, and tomorrow came after one long day and a long, long night. 'Bowie', as promised, produced the list after prayers and started to read. For the first time I was glad that my name was Banton, so with him reading in alphabetical order I didn't have long to wait to learn my fate – I had made it. I ran home at lunchtime like an Olympic-class runner to see what my parents thought of the sealed envelope. I was on my way to Guild Street Central School.

The school summer holidays passed and I was starting on a period where life simply took off. All dressed up in my green cap and blazer, I waited for my pal, Gilbert Hewitt (from the shop in Waterloo Street), and with satchels around our necks, off we went. The school is now used as offices etc. and stands opposite the cinema in Guild Street. Boys were upstairs and girls downstairs – no co-education or co-habitation then.

We were divided into A and B forms and into four 'houses' for sport etc. I was in A form and Rodney house, as was the blond lad from the rugby match, Clem Whiles. We were to become the closest of friends throughout our school lives, and I have recently remade contact with him in Canada.

This school was all I dreamed of. In the old library building in Union Street (now demolished) we had a joinery workshop, physics laboratory, massive modern studio and, right on the top floor, a chemistry laboratory and lecture room. We were the best-equipped school in town. Further, we had a good cricket coach named Lawley. Bookkeeping, shorthand and French were compulsory. along with the 'three Rs'. Typing was optional in one's own time before school.

At this stage of my life, my grandfather's death became a disturbing factor. As a means of compensation, Bass had paid my grandmother for office cleaning in the early hours of the mornings, with brewers' white coats to launder at home.

The laundering developed into private laundering for several of the heads of Bass and fellow brewers Worthington's, which replaced the early morning cleaning. By the time I started at Guild Street I had inherited, due to the ill-health of my step-grandfather, the task of collecting and delivering this work. This meant that I had errands to do during dinnertime, after school and on Saturdays.

With plenty of homework and a growing activity in sport, this chore was a bind to say the least. I wondered why I had to do this and other kids didn't (this carried on even after I started work), although it had its compensation in the form of tips.

At Christmas time, my grandmother and mother would have a lorry-load of turkeys and geese etc. from Bass, which they would pluck and dress to become Christmas boxes for all the heads of department. This would entail them working through most of the night, meaning that my mother would be missing from home for a few days. (This was essential because there were no such things as fridges for us then.) The front room floor at 5 Blackpool Street was cleared to receive the dressed birds awaiting collection, and I would deliver to those who lived in the vicinity – and many did, in Blackpool Street and Branstone Road. I would sometimes pick up as much in tips as my father earned in a couple of weeks, and this used to buy Christmas presents for my sisters and on a couple of occasions paid the rates which were due on 31 December. I was pleased about this because it meant we all had a happy Christmas.

Then came the unsavoury side of the deal. We had obtained some wooden barrels which the greengrocer had received his apples in. These had been filled with all the stinking 'innards' of the poultry, and as each one was filled I had to take it round the corner to the destructor. Through the gates at the end of Watson Street (where you entered *Bondend* Tip) was an uphill road where the refuse lorries would go and tip their load over the end of a huge ever-burning fire. I would dispose of these stinking barrels in the same way, and was glad it was so close to Blackpool Street. The feathers and down were wrapped in clean newspaper (saved up for weeks) and stored away in a disused coal shed, and would be fetched by a firm to be made into pillows and bedding.

Although I was not aware of it at the time, the pattern of my future was now being made.

One house to which I delivered laundry was No. 63 Branstone Road, the home of Mr Lyons, who was head chemist at Worthington's Brewery. It was a combination of his efforts and those of Mr A. Barrington (the head brewer) that made Worthington's ales so famous.

Like all scientists, he was very impulsive and erratic, but he was always very kind to me if he was home when I called. His son was a teacher at our woodwork school, and from him he had learned that I had gained good marks at chemistry. When I was due to leave school, on one of my visits to No. 63, quite out of the blue, Mr Lyon came into the kitchen and asked me if I would like to go and work in his laboratory – a chance in a lifetime, a job.

I joined Worthington's, but the vacancy was not available for three months so I was given a temporary job in another department and when the time came I decided to stay where I was.

Another house I visited was on the corner of Lichfield Street, which is now occupied by a team of medical consultants. This was the home of Mr Stoner, a retired master from the Grammar School – at this time in Bond Street. It was a large, old-fashioned house with library and art studio. Mr Stoner, who kept a huge collection of butterflies, stuffed birds and bird eggs at the top of the house, lived with his daughter Muriel. They employed a housekeeper, Mrs Early, who lived in Blackpool Street.

Mrs Early always wore a black outfit, from her bonnet down to her laced-up boots, and always appeared to be running as she hurried along with little short steps. My grandmother would say: 'There goes Mrs Early – late again.'

The daughter was, I guess, in her early 30s, a really beautiful, dark-haired woman. She was an actress by profession and spent her spare time in her art studio. Whilst I waited in there one day, I gazed at some of her paintings and she noticed that I was interested. Many times from then on, when I was in a hurry to get off to other activities, I would have to show a polite interest as she described to me her latest works. I should have kept my nose out in the first place!

Time was going on, and my schooling was taking its course. I was in the soccer team and the cricket team, and enjoyed the cross-country runs. Our sports field was the 'Ox-hay' for one half-session per week, but team practice took place after school hours. If it were not for the errands I had to run, I am sure that my education and sports would have benefited. However, that was the way of life in the circumstances of the time.

Whilst at Guild Street School, we would, during break time, watch the demolition of Burton Opera House and the building of the Ritz Cinema (later the Odeon) on its site. Italian workmen came to lay the terrazzo floor in the foyer.

On several occasions we had difficulty getting to school due to flooding of the streets. Brook Street, Guild Street and Station Street were particularly vulnerable. Station Street was surfaced with wooden blocks, and during the floods these became huge rafts and we would try to get from one to the other – often failing.

The headmaster was C.E. ('Chaser') Binns, who would stand at the door of his office as we went upstairs, watching for unpolished shoes, ties not properly worn, late arrivals etc.

One master was A.P. ('Doffey') Bakewell. Built like Geoff Capes, he taught book-keeping, shorthand etc., and in his spare time was a lay-preacher. If you performed any misdemeanour in his class, his hand would land like a side of frozen beef in your ear and all the bells in Burton would ring for half an hour. If you ducked, he would put his foot and his 18-stone-plus weight on your foot to make sure he got you second time. He didn't have much trouble with his classes! If you forgot to date your work, Doffey would turn your book upside down and write through as many pages as he could 'on Thursday the thirteenth day of the month of May, in the year of our Lord one thousand etc.', and you have to rewrite the lot before his lesson. Happy days nevertheless.

On one occasion we borrowed the cricket field of Trumans, which was where the Lloyds foundry is now built, and we hosted a school from Nottingham. The groundsman was Bert Fitzgerald, whom I knew quite well, and when Clem Whiles and I went out to open the innings, he said he would give us half-a–crown if we could hit the pavilion clock. A little later, I saw Clem laugh as the bowler came in and I knew immediately what he had in mind, and I was right – he missed the clock but put the ball on the roof and Bert shouted: 'The bet's off!'

While my personal life was happy enough, this was of course the early 1930s and the time of the Great Depression. Thousands of people were out of work, and those in work were poorly paid. Despite these conditions, or perhaps because of them, there was a wonderful spirit among people. Neighbours would share a pot of tea in order not to waste it. One could, and did, leave your house unlocked and it would be safe, and leave your cycle (if you had one) in the street and it would come to no harm.

We at No. 11, and our neighbours, each had the luxury of a WC which was built onto the back of the house. Many houses had pan-toilets (not even chemical) which were emptied during the night by council 'night-soil men' with horse-drawn vehicles. My Uncle Sam's house was one such. There was a building at the bottom of our garden, which had an open front, in which stood the dustbins of No. 10 and No. 11. On either end was a small place which used to be the dry lavatory and was now used as the garden shed. All people had coal fires, and the dustman would come along with a tin bath and empty the refuse, ashes and all, into it, and lift it onto his padded head. Off he would go, spilling it along the garden path, down the 'entry' to tip what he had left into an open cart standing on the road and leave you to sweep up after him. No one hung any washing out until he had been.

Washday started at about 5am when Father rose to prepare for a 6 am start at the brewery. He would light the copper fire. The copper, which stood in a corner of the kitchen, was a brick-built construction with a fire hole underneath a huge iron cauldron, and the degree of success in the lighting of it was dependent entirely on the direction of the wind. Mother would use a brewery cask (a kilderkin, holding 18 gallons and weighing about ½ cwt) as a wash tub and huge wooden dolly-pegs to agitate the wash. After wringing and then a rinse in Reckitts Blue water, she would wind it through a huge mangle with large wooden rollers, turned by means of a wheel of about 3ft diameter. This performance, and cleaning up afterwards, was a long day's hard work.

We were among the first people in Victoria Street to have electric lighting under a scheme devised by the council, who owned both the gas and electric works (Electric Street, where the power station was, is off Wetmore Road). It was wonderful to be fully lighted, as only the main rooms had gas-light of any quality and even this was no comparison to electric. A two-way switch on the staircase, which had no previous lighting, was magic.

The first wireless we had was operated by an accumulator, which was a wet battery requiring charging every week. A huge pole was erected at the bottom of the garden and the aerial ran from it into the house.

As for shopping, the numerous small shops would sell 2oz of cheese or margarine, an odd slice of bacon, and treacle or jam loose if you took an empty jar along. I used to be fascinated to watch the men in the larger shops packing up orders. They would place a sheet of brown paper on the counter, stack the goods on it and, as quick as a conjurer, fold it into a neat parcel and tie it with string, having reckoned the cost in the process.

The famous Jarrow Hunger Marchers, who walked from the north of England to London to protest at their poverty, paused in Burton for rest and food. They spent a night in the St Paul's Institute, which has since been demolished but which stood alongside the church. There was much apprehension as to what might happen, Burton being a strong Tory seat and the working population not having much sympathy for the marchers. Some shop windows along the route were boarded up, but in the event it was all well behaved and went off peacefully.

The 'Means Test' was in force, which meant that before one could get any dole, any articles such as non-essential furniture, bicycles etc. had to be sold; men would go to great lengths to conceal a bicycle as it was the only transport to assist in searching for work. Some of the buildings which are now in use as offices at the District Hospital were part of a complex known as Belvedere House, which was a poor-house. The allotments alongside were used to grow food for the inmates – all local, destitute people. When labour was required on this project, the dole office would send men there. In return for their toil they would receive tickets to purchase food, thus the place became known as 'The Workhouse'.

There were many vagrants walking up and down the country, living by begging or doing any menial job they could manage in return for food or a few coppers – or even an old jacket or something. If any of these unfortunates were in town, the local council was bound to give them one night's, and only one, shelter. If they had any money on them, this would be taken as payment, so if they were so fortunate they would hide it under a hedge or somewhere. To this day, in one of those buildings there are two iron rings, one at either end. At night, a rope was attached between them and these poor vagrants would hang with their arms over the rope and sleep standing up. Thus the council had fulfilled its obligation (and hence the saying 'could sleep on a clothes-line').

I have memories of my father taking me to see the widening of Trent Bridge, and also to the Ox Hay when the Trent was frozen over. There were hundreds of people skating right across the river, and others with braziers selling toasted chestnuts and popcorn. Normally the river was a haven for swimmers, and a large row of bathing-huts stood along the banks here.

Renwick & Hunt's had a bakery at the top of Victoria Street and a grocery shop and warehouse in Albert Street (now Timboard). We used to follow the carts home at night and would buy a large bag of leftover cakes for 2d.

One lunchtime, my father, coming home for his dinner, turned into Victoria Street and saw one of the horses down in its shafts and men hitting it in an attempt to get it to its feet. Dad dropped his lunch-basket and ran, cleared the men away, took off his coat and put it over the horse's head. At this, the horse simply rose to its feet and Dad calmed it down while at the same time giving the men a few verbals. He certainly could handle horses – all 5ft 6in of him.

Uncle Sam bought a beautiful young horse and got my Dad to help him train it. When the time was ready, Dad got up early one Sunday, put the horse into its harness and trap and took it around Anslow and home again without incident. On the Monday evening, Uncle Sam and a friend tried this, but at Derby Turn the horse took fright, smashed up the trap and cleared a petrol pump off the front of Kennings' newly built petrol station. My father played hell and sent me to the chemists for bandages etc. to treat the horse. In good weather, the horse was kept in fields on Rolleston Road (opposite St Andrew's Drive), and Dad would take me up there with apples and crusts for him; one whistle and the horse would come at full gallop as if from nowhere. When we left, we would hear the horse whinny after us as we walked away along the road.

When youngsters, we could safely play in the streets as cars were few and far between – and not very fast. As a matter of fact, I was one of the lucky kids who had a ride in a car. Miss Muriel, the daughter of the landlord of the Lord Napier, fetched me home from the infirmary in a bull-nosed Morris which had a 'dickie seat' (like a car boot) at the back for two people.

On Saturdays, two or three of us would go to watch the Burton Town play on The Crescent. We would each earn or cadge two pence; we would pool this, as admission was one penny and the remainder would be spent half on sweets to share and the rest to buy raffle tickets at one pence each as the match ball would be raffled at half time – called 'Penny on the ball'. Cox's Silver Prize Band would march from King Edward Place and, followed by supporters, would play before the match and at half time. The highlight was when 'The Town' had a good FA Cup run and First Division side Blackburn Rovers came to play them. Blackburn won 4-0, and I was to meet one of their players some years later in Malaya.

One of the schoolboy antics I was involved with was the moving of Mr Ford's bean-sticks. Mr Ford, the neighbour of one of the gang, was a keen gardener. He had erected the sticks and planted seeds at each one. We decided to move the sticks, wholesale, about a couple of feet further back and had to wait until late in the evening for darkness. After much religious watering and waiting, Mr Ford was completely foxed when the inevitable happened – or rather didn't happen. It was after I came home from the war when, with my father, I took Grandad Fitzjohn to the Napier for a drink, that I solved the mystery which had caused 'Old Pen Ford' a deal of leg pulling over many years.

The pub was in uproar, and none enjoyed it more than 'Old Pen Ford', and Grandad – who was in his element anyway because 'Our Jim' had taken him in – laughed so much that his huge paunch shook his gold watch chain.

I can still see him wiping the tears of happiness from his eyes and his beer from his beard. Such a little treat meant the whole world to a grand old fellow who used to wait daily on his doorstep to see if my mother had a letter from me; they were always passed to him to read later.

One frightening moment of my school days came as I was walking along Derby Street with a lad named Bill Topliss (Bill lived at No. 9 and later also became a PoW in Singapore – another coincidence in life). It came on to rain and thunder, and we started to run for home. There was one terrific crack and flash, and we saw a ball of flame bounce slowly off the road and push some brickwork off the corner of Truman's brewery. The rain fell in torrents as a score or so of sparrows flew past about a foot off the ground and a hot breeze wafted by.

So, as four years passed with school, homework, errands and the usual pastimes of childhood, I was reaching school-leaving age. I acquired a fairly good all-round education without attaining academic heights. To this day, I am sure I would have had better results but for the time I had to spend running errands. However, the times demanded such things, I am content that I played my part and in retrospect I find that I gained other qualities as a result.

Halfway through my schooling at Guild Street, I was making no progress in the French class and at the end of the school year I was sent along to see Mr Binns, the headmaster – that meant trouble. I knocked on the door and was called in. 'Chaser' looked at me and said, 'Sit down laddie' – everyone was 'laddie' to him. He went on to say that he thought I was trying too hard and allowing it to worry me. After a little chat, he took all my books from me, and told me to go on holiday and forget about it. This I did, and it certainly worked because after the holiday it all became much easier. 'Chaser' wasn't such a tyrant after all.

The other, non-academic side of my life was altering too, and among my recreation was Derby Street Chapel and its activities. The main attractions were badminton, table tennis, rambles and boating trips on the Trent. Although I did not join the Boys' Brigade, I played in its football team, and that team was again to play a major part in my destiny – and a happy part it turned out to be. (The Boys' Brigade was a youth movement, similar to the Scouts. They had a marching band and a uniform of navy-blue and white.)

Apart from football, I was also keen on and a bit useful at cricket. Next door to my Grandmother and living at No. 4 Blackpool Street was Jimmy Eden and his family. Jimmy was a member of Burton Rugby Club and gained many county caps. He was also a member of Everards' boys' cricket team, and he persuaded me to do a little job for them. On match days I was to go to the brewery in Anglesey Road (now Heritage Brewery), collect a truck on which was a pin (4½ gallons) of beer and a box of sandwiches etc. for the players' teas, and take it to the ground in Blackpool Street.

This was something I really enjoyed, because not only was I rewarded financially with a generous whip-round each time, but I was amongst cricketers.

Everards was only a small company and often had to scratch to raise eleven players, so I soon found myself getting an odd game, then the odd game became a regular one – and I was getting paid as well!

The great day came when I was to play in the Breweries Cup match against Eadies. At this time, the Breweries Cup was THE event of Burton's summer. It was a hospital charity event, and everyone bought tickets (6d each), even if they were not interested in cricket. The hospitals were dependent on these charities; if one fell ill, you would get a 'recommend' from your brewery to say you had donated, and you would take this to the hospital with you. All the breweries competed – the larger ones each had one professional player, and Everards were the complete outsiders. Keeping wicket for Eadies was Ian Chambers, still hale and hearty today and well over 80 years old, and we managed to beat them on the Blackpool Street ground. Ian was my mother's stepbrother. In the next round we had to play Allsopps, who played on Meadow Road and had three Jones brothers (Aunt Elsie's brothers), and we got trounced. But it was wonderful to me, and I am certain that I am the only person to play in the competition whilst still at school. Ian Botham never had such fame or happiness!

Another great cricket match was when we entertained the police one evening. The rain poured down and not one ball was bowled. The beer and food was taken care of, and much fun was made of a very popular copper of his day, PC Johnson Cartwright. He couldn't stand Gorgonzola cheese, and after numerous tricks had been pulled on him it came time to disperse. In fading light and pouring rain, the coppers set off across the field, carrying their gear in large holdalls, two men to each. Someone shouted to inform 'Copper Cartwright' that his bag contained cheese for his supper, whereupon, having had his ample share of the brew, he proceeded to empty his bag in the pouring rain onto the ground. His mates were not amused, but everyone else was.

This may seem an everyday joke, but to me it was the start of my adult life, and against the background of life at the time it was a whole new world. I was enjoying it to the full.

Another character of those days was an ex-professional cricketer, Arthur Wragg. He stood well over 6ft tall, with a fine slim, athletic physique. Arthur was 'the doctor's man'. He would call on people and collect 2d or 3d per week, which would entitle them to the services of a doctor. With his rolled brolly, dark suit and a white pocket-handkerchief, he always walked his rounds, and his area was Burton, Tutbury, Branston and Barton, etc. After he discovered that I was interested in cricket, he would always have one of his experiences to relate and pass on a few tips, so I suppose I owe him something too.

The last week of school saw us handing in books to each master as we attended our final session with them, and only two of them made any occasion of this event.

Mr Sauvain, the French master, sitting at his desk, spoke to each of us in turn. He was always a jovial character, and lived at the round bungalow on Rolleston Road.

To me he recalled the incident of two years previously when I went to visit 'Chaser', and said that he had also learned something from that. Mr Sauvain (known as Sawbones) had always been kind to a couple of lads from the 'Boys Home' (an orphanage situated in what is now part of the District Hospital), and he entertained them at his home on some weekends. One of these lads, Jimmy England, had left at the previous end of term to join the Navy. Due to some slip-up, Jim had to return to us, but he had destroyed all his books. This left poor old England on the end of much humorous torment from Sauvain, and this was the theme of his final chat. Sauvain concluded: 'Whatever happens to us we will always have England's Navy to see us through.' Little did he know how true those words would be in five years' time.

Taffy Jones ('Jones the history') was the other teacher to mark the end of our time at school. For a while now, Hitler had been causing some gossip and First World War veterans were forecasting another war if his antics were not checked – the outcome is now common history.

Taffy brought it to our minds just what was happening. Until now it had not been of much interest to us, but at length he explained the 1918 Armistice agreement and how this Hitler bloke was contravening it, and the possible consequences.

As we left, he shook each one of us by the hand and wished us well for the future, and I am sure he had a good idea of what it would be.

On the last afternoon, 'Charlie' Binns had us all together to tell us how fortunate we had been to attend his fine school, and hoped that we would always be a credit to it.

And off we went!

PS: The first air raid on Germany was commanded by Squadron Leader Staton, an ex-Guild Street scholar who led three Wellington bombers to the Kiel Canal. I met him in Java when he was Air Commodore and drove him 80 miles from Kalidjati to Batavia, and he made certain I had enough money to stay well looked-after overnight.

Chapter 3

School to War

Upon leaving school I was one of the fortunate ones who had a job to go to, and life soon took on a new dimension.

My father called me at 5am, as work at breweries started at 6 am, but earlier during busy seasons. The 48-hour week comprised five days of 6am to 4pm, with half an hour for breakfast and one hour for dinner, and Saturday from 6am to noon, with a half-hour breakfast.

The first job I had was stencilling codes on casks, and upon arriving for my first day I was taken to the mess room and seated at a table for six. Two of my tablemates were Stan Brotherhood, who was wicketkeeper for the brewery team, and Frank Dawson, who was a well-known local boxer, which delighted me.

My wages were eighteen shillings per week, of which I kept eight and my mother had ten. As my father's wage was little over £2 when he was not on short-time, the financial situation at home was much improved. With my share, I was well able to clothe myself and have money in my pocket – and buy my books for night school.

It seemed that everything changed at once. I had more friends and more interests, one of which was the motor racing at Donnington, which was the first road-racing circuit in the world pre-war. The world's top drivers came there, and I saw them all. Later, when Frank Tricklebank became 17, he passed the newly introduced driving test and his Dad used to trust him to borrow his new Flying Standard car to take us to the meetings – we were the first of the Yuppies!

The front room at home had stood empty for some time since Uncle Bill went to live with Grandma in Blackpool Street, and now that better times had arrived, it was possible for us to have it furnished. One of my closest friends, Vic Reed, and I stripped it, and with help redecorated it. Came the day when the furniture arrived, my mother was beside herself with joy.

The lads and lasses at Derby Street Chapel were all growing up, and we used to organise rambles, coach trips, fancy-dress parties, etc. One of my favourites was when we would hire a fleet of rowing boats or canoes from Dobson's by the Ferry Bridge, then go up as far as Walton and picnic, sometimes returning after dark. There used to be a weir at Drakelow, where we had to haul the boats out of the water, drag them along and re-launch them on the other side.

Some of the older members of the Boys' Brigade and a few of our friends formed a football club and decided to call it Burton Orient. We played anyone who would give us a game and applied to join the Burton and District League, but were told we were too young. The following season we took on any league team with a spare date, and at the next AGM enough of them gave us their vote and we were elected. Our results were such that on Saturday evenings my Dad would ask, 'How many today?' – the result was a foregone conclusion.

One of the fundraising efforts for our club was a concert in February 1938 in the schoolroom of Moseley Street Chapel (now used by the Salvation Army). Among the performers was a small band of three youths and one girl violinist. I was the doorman, and after the band had opened the concert, the girl came to ask me what time they would be on again as she was also playing at George Street the same evening.

I'd had one-off dates before, but girls who did not play cricket or football failed to stir me. Although I did not expect this girl to play these games either, something happened to me in that short conversation and I was most disappointed when she walked home with a couple of the youths. I told my mate Vic about this and he just laughed – as he always did

At dinner time the next day, I asked my Dad what he thought of the concert and his reply was, 'Who was the young lass you were talking to last night?' He did not believe me when I said I didn't know, but he had, I learned later, said to my mother, 'You have seen your daughter-in-law tonight.' Events proved him right.

Vic got all Dorothy Mason's details from her pal, Kath Dewey (now married to Freddie Lester, a milkman), and arranged a meeting for us. I thought this was a leg-pull on his part, but he said he would wait with me until she came, so we met on the corner of Waterloo Street and Albert Street on a Saturday evening. With Dorothy was Patch the dog, because his walk was her excuse for being out. However, he was returned home, and Dorothy and I walked around the streets getting to know each other. I learned that one of the lads with whom she had walked home from the chapel concert was her brother Lawrence – so that hurdle was out of the way.

On Saturdays I would work from 6am until noon, then dash to Kinds before their 12.30pm closure, fill two bags of sawdust and with a couple of the lads go over the Outwoods Rec and mark out the pitch. Then it was home for a snack, back to St Margaret's schoolroom at the back of the church in Shobnall Street (now demolished, opposite Kinds) to carry the posts over to the pitch, play the match, return the posts, home for tea and off to the cinema with the lads. As showers had not been thought of, we had half a dozen butts (100-gallon casks) cut into halves, and cousin Cecil used to stoke the copper and have hot water ready for us. Aunty Elsie, who lived close by, provided a white enamel bucket full of hot milk, and as such we were one of the better cared for clubs in our league.

Now that Dorothy was on the scene, it was a case of off to a different cinema than the lads, but often all was not well. After such a hectic day, the warmth of the cinema tended to send me to sleep; Dorothy was not amused but a bag of chocolates would ease her sufferance.

I was enjoying work at the brewery and starting to earn some overtime and make new friends. Among these were Cyril Fletcher, Les Mortimer and Ken Rowley; the latter two lived in Stanton Road, Les being married and Ken living with his married sister. Dorothy and I would be invited to parties at both these homes, and would walk up there and back again after midnight. There was no alternative.

During this time, a tragedy jolted us for a while when one of our Orient players, Laurie Pearson, died fairly suddenly from tuberculosis. His funeral took place on the morning of the first Saturday of the 1937–38 season, and some of our lads acted as bearers, a job for which lots were drawn as everyone had volunteered. 'Lol' had played for us throughout the previous season, and had only been ill for about four weeks. It was his mother's wish that our match should not be cancelled, and I was picked to play in his position. Playing on the opposite wing to my normal position, I had an experience which sent me cold and I began to believe in things over which we have no control. As I tried to centre a ball, I hit it with the outside of my foot (not intentionally), and it curled in to become a wonder goal which I was certain was scored by 'Lol' Pearson.

Another incident in this vein happened when I had a new bike. As I was leaving home, I was putting a clean handkerchief into my pocket and my mother said, 'Unfold it or you will have bad luck.' I laughed and went out. At the junction of Edward Street and Waterloo Street, I ran into a tram and my bike lost the contest. I became so superstitious, but years later I had to say 'to hell with all this superstition' and changed my thoughts on such matters.

Dorothy and I were becoming closer to each other, and she became the first and only girly whom I ever took home.

Dorothy lived at 78A Victoria Crescent, where she was born, and had one brother, Lawrence, who was six years older. Her father, Jack, was a sawyer at Kinds in Shobnall Street, and her mother, May, was a kind-hearted lady with a good sense of humour. Mrs Mason was always smart in appearance, and walked with such grace and dignity that I came later to refer to her as 'the Duchess'. They had met whilst in service at Wildboarclough in Cheshire and came back to Burton – where Mrs Mason had been born May Weston – after losing their first-born owing to lack of attention due to the isolation of 'The Clough'. Dorothy's mother, like mine, was a cook.

Although we did not know it, Dorothy had been at Grange Street School at the time I was, and she then went on to Goodman Street. By the time I met her, she had become quite an accomplished violinist.

Often on Saturday evenings, we would return to 78A, where Uncle Len and Aunty Gladys (May's sister) would be. We would start playing darts etc., and Lawrence and his pals would often join us later and the piano would come into its own. We had many happy hours like this.

Dorothy's mother had three sisters – Rosa, Ethel and Gladys – and one brother, Will.

Aunty Rosa, mother of Sheila, Eileen and Eric Gee (a name you can see in the church at 'The Clough'), had a harder life than any of us. Her husband deserted her and the small children in the days when there was no assistance for people in these circumstances. The things Rosa did in order to prevent the authorities taking her family from her or splitting them up into the care of relations you will find hard to believe. Not only did Rosa tackle any work she could get – delivering milk with horse and float, selling ice cream from a tricycle, working in service; you name it, Aunty Rosa did it, and would not accept charity from anyone – but she often slept out in the open to hide her children if she had an idea that the authorities were coming to take them away. Rosa kept her family intact, and despite a very hard life she lived to be over 90.

Aunty Ethel married Lionel Tyler and lived in Uxbridge Street, and they had two daughters, Doris and Barbara. Dorothy spent many happy childhood days with her cousins, and Aunty Ethel would take her with them on outings and day trips to the seaside. By the time I met Dorothy, the Tyler family had moved to Northampton, where Uncle Lionel had become head of a wagon-repair shop (rail wagons of course).

In later years when we owned a car, we would visit Northampton regularly to see Dorothy's favourite aunt. As Uncle Lionel had been a keen cricketer in his early days but had no son of his own, he appeared to look on me as a substitute. We would sit and chat, while three females tried to drown us out! We enjoyed these trips and the bond still remains to this day, although Aunty Ethel and Uncle Lionel have long since passed on.

Aunty Gladys was a tailoress who married the son of her boss and became Mrs Len Rodgers. They had no children and carried on the business until Uncle Len was, 70. Being childless, they looked after Len's brother Edgar and his Aunty Sylvia, and later a wartime pal of Len's named John Smith. All these people were Methodists and were active members of Moseley Street Chapel, and after its closure Belvedere Road Chapel. Dorothy was their favourite niece, and I later became the odd job man at 147 Shobnall Street for decorating, etc.

The brother was Uncle Will Weston, a rosy faced outdoor fiend, as tough as old boots but as gentle as a lamb. By the time I met him he had a smallholding at Fradley, where he lived with his wife, Millie, and two daughters, Marjorie and Brenda. As well as his smallholding, on which Millie also worked, he had a job at the Branston factory, and also found time to give piano lessons. Earlier in his life he had been in the Army. He was a wonderful musician and was trained at Kneller Hall, which was a top Army music academy. I remember one Saturday lunchtime he called at 78A to collect food scraps for his pigs, and as one of his daughters was about to be married, he sat with pencil and paper and wrote the music as it was played on the radio (pre tape-recorder days). Although his knuckles by now were swollen with arthritis, he still played beautifully. He could play any musical instrument, and at 70 years old he marched around Wembley Stadium playing a trombone at a rally of Jehovah's Witnesses. No wonder Dorothy played in a BBC broadcast at the age of 12 with Swadlincote Junior Band. Dorothy and I, along with her Uncle Ian, often cycled to Fradley in those pre-war days.

Dorothy's father had one brother and one sister. The brother, Lawrence, was a coach painter and sign writer with a bus company in Manchester, and was married to Alice. They had a son, also Lawrence, who lives at Chapel-en-le-Frith, and a daughter, Marina, who lives at Macclesfield. Mrs Mossall and her husband have two daughters and one son, and came home a day early from holiday in Switzerland to come to our Ruby Wedding anniversary.

The sister, Gertrude, married Jack Harrison and they had three daughters, who we last knew as living in Nottingham. Jack would mend anything from cars to watches, and had a wood yard on Derby Road before moving to a place called Fishponds near Nottingham. He bought an old building and put some homemade machinery in it, and made and sold coat hangers, brush heads and such like. He also built a bungalow alongside the business premises in his spare time; when we last visited it, although they were all living in it, there was only half the roof on and he was constantly in trouble with the authorities over it.

All these people had known hard times, and it was only due to the gathering war clouds that life became easier due to more work. The old saying applied: 'It's an ill wind that blows no good.'

Due to Dorothy's parents being older than mine, her brother being six years older than herself and no girls of her age living nearby, Dorothy did not have a childhood like mine. School, violin practice and running errands seemed to be her lot. So when she came to No. 11, where gangs of my pals were in and out and my sisters were around, she enjoyed it. The lads taught her how to drink pop from a bottle and the vinegar from the bottom of a chip bag. Although such things had never been approved of by her mother, when she eventually heard about it, it appealed to her sense of impish humour and gave her a laugh. Having said that, it must not be forgotten that there was always a warm welcome for anyone at No. 78A and I enjoyed going there just as much. I have many happy memories of her parents, and as this story unfolds you will learn what wonderful people they were who later became my mother and father-in-law.

In the autumn of 1938 came the crisis when Prime Minister Neville Chamberlain postponed the outbreak of war with his 'Peace in our time' mission to Munich. With Britain forced to prepare itself for the coming war, everyone appeared to be breaking out of their financial depression. We younger ones seemed determined to enjoy it and ignore the inevitable as we carried on happily as we were.

At Christmas of 1938, Dorothy's family were set to visit No. 11 for the first time on Boxing Day. During the morning, Burton Orient played a match at Tutbury against Tutbury St Mary's. We hired a small bus owned by a man from Rangemore, and took with us some sherry for a drink on the way home – a long journey. Some of the lads had left their bikes at No. 11, and thus it transpired that more than half the team finished up there. There was plenty of port wine and sherry to share, and as my mother enjoyed crowds of laughing youngsters, out came the mince pies etc. and it became open house. However, when at last they all departed, my mother and sisters had to start baking again!

The Masons and the Rodgers joined the Bantons and friends, and with Lol (Dorothy's brother) at the piano, the singing and drinking went on until about 5am the following morning. I left with Dorothy and her family to make sure that they got home safely (that was my excuse anyway). We bade farewell to Uncle Ian and Aunty Gladys at the corner of Edward Street, and on our way along Victoria Crescent, Dorothy's Dad – who always had a fit of the giggles when he had a drink – said that we had either come the wrong way or the crescent was longer than it used to be. We had all had a good time on what was to be the last peaceful Christmas for six years.

As we entered 1939, the prosperity of war preparations meant that many people for the first time in their lives had a few shillings to spare. As shortages, which were to be experienced later, were not yet with us, the older people broke out from the years of depression and dire poverty. The young ones turned a blind eye to the daunting future and appeared to adopt the attitude of 'enjoy it while it lasts and worry about it tomorrow when it comes'.

I, for my part, enjoyed my work and my sport, and Dorothy and I began to discuss the prospect of us getting engaged.

During the late summer of 1939, I went along with Vic Reed and Frank Trickleback to join the RAF Reserves at Burnaston – they as pilots, I as an observer (later known as navigators). Pilots were given priority, and before an observer course was filled, war was declared and I was later advised to volunteer again.

Came the morning of Sunday, 3 September 1939. Germany had invaded Poland and a deadline for cessation of hostilities, which had been handed to them, was now expired. It was a warm and sunny morning, and I was ready to go round to see Dorothy, but I waited in the backyard to hear the declaration of war at 11am. I returned to the house to say 'cheerio' to my mum and dad. Mum just looked at me and said, 'Cheerio lad!', and my Dad said, 'So now we know lad – off you go and see Dorothy.' It was a scene which I have recalled on many occasions since, under various conditions and under many different skies. I now know fully what thoughts were going through their minds, and that it was better that I left them alone for a while.

I arrived at 78A to find that Joe had done the same, and Dorothy's Dad was at work (an unusual occasion but a sign of the times). Dorothy's Mum spoke a few words about all the young lads who would have to go, and as she said 'Let's hope it is over soon', her voice failed and she retreated to the kitchen in tears. After a few minutes, she came back with cups of tea and we did not return to the subject.

'Big Jim', a retired Royal Marine with 23 years' service who had married the daughter from No. 10, had already been recalled to the Colours. Vic and Frank were to report forthwith, and first of all were doing full-time flying training at Burnaston. The TA and Yeomanry were taken into the full-time forces. Local buildings were taken over and troops were moving into them, and so it was until Christmas.

This was the beginning of what came to be known as the 'Phoney War'. Nothing much was happening, except at sea, where we were losing a number of ships to German U-boats and bombers. Britain was hastily building ships, planes, tanks, etc., and everyone was working all hours of day and night. The Home Guard was being formed, and ARP wardens and members of the Auxiliary Fire Service were being recruited.

At Christmas, Dorothy and I were to be engaged. For what reason I don't know, we had left the buying of our ring until the last day, which was a Saturday, and Saturday of course was match day.

I was at work from 5am until 1pm, and in the afternoon we played Burton Town Reserves on The Crescent, with Dorothy and both of our families in the stand. The plan was for Dorothy and I to go by bus into town for our ring immediately after the match. Due to blackout restrictions, shops had to close early, so the schedule was, to say the least, very tight. However, I was to pay the price for previous youthful pranks.

There was a very jolly, moustachioed old chap at the brewery who worked in the joinery department, and we lads would go to fetch wood to start our office fires. We used to plague this chap something rotten, and he secretly, I'm sure, enjoyed it; we didn't always win by any means. By now Jimmy Wood (an apt name!) was retired and had a spare-time job stoking the boiler and looking after the changing rooms at The Crescent, and when I dashed off the pitch he had played his ace. I couldn't find my clothes, while my shoelaces had hundreds of knots in them. The delay was almost catastrophic, and could have changed the course of my life.

Dorothy and I dashed to Postles Jewellers in Station Street and arrived just as they were putting up the wooden shutters to close. We already knew which ring we wanted, but another five minutes and a beautiful romance could have been ended. 'You and your damned football!' was a phrase I recall from the inquest.

We all made the best of Christmas, and apart from getting engaged the highlight was when we all gathered at No. 11 for a party, again on Boxing Day, again with plenty to eat and drink, and again well into the morning of

27 December. Little did we know that Christmas 1939 would be the last one we would spend together until 1945 – and then only just.

Although the holiday was only two days off work, we had to catch up by working more overtime. Dorothy was making Wellington boots at BTR, and these were in great demand by the forces – everyone was affected in some way or other.

Things were getting more disrupted on the social front; with lads joining up, working for longer hours etc., football clubs were folding and local-based forces teams were taking up their fixtures. Cinemas were also closing early.

The winter was severe, adding to the experience of our first blackouts. Although there were no cars parked in the streets in those days, I remember crossing the road in Victoria Crescent on my way to visit Dorothy one evening. Trying to find the kerb on the far side, I fell over a bicycle which someone had propped up there. Apart from all else, I had ruined a perfectly good pair of grey flannels and not improved the appearance of my 'Mac'. Thus incensed, I picked up the cycle and dropped it over the fence into Mr Richards' front garden, then I knocked on the door and said a few words. The Richards were very good friends of the Masons, and Avril's daughter Lynda married my nephew Brian Burton many years later.

In late February, I learned that the RAF recruiting centre in the Assembly Rooms at Derby was accepting volunteers (the façade of this building has been preserved and stands in the Crich Tramway Museum near Matlock). Cyril Fletcher and I took an afternoon off work and went over to join up. It was a bitterly cold day, with a blizzard blowing, but we got signed up so considered our trip worthwhile.

A few days later we were instructed to report to Derby en route for RAF Cardington, the former airship base in Bedfordshire and home of the 'Barrage Balloon'. Coming so soon after our engagement, Dorothy was not at all pleased. However, we paid our farewells to our mates at work on Tuesday as we were to be away early on the Wednesday morning. Tuesday evening was also time to say a temporary farewell to Dorothy and her Mum and Dad.

After spending all day Wednesday in crowded and freezing trains and stations, we arrived at Cardington in the evening, tired, hungry and cold. We were given a meal of sorts and shown to our billets, which were long wooden huts without heating, and here we spent the longest and coldest night of my life – before or since. Thursday and Friday were spent queuing for food in icy winds and blizzards, listening to lectures on the rudiments of the RAF and witnessing a scene of utter chaos. Many blokes passed out under the conditions and a number of volunteers went home rather than join up.

On Friday afternoon the volunteers were sworn in, given the 'King's Shilling' and sent home on 'Deferred Service' to be called back later. The conscripted people had no option but to stay!

At 9am on Saturday, Cyril and I were in the office of our boss Walter Goodhead. 'I thought you had gone to help the Royal Air Force win the war,' he said. To this, Cyril answered: 'You always taught us to rush the job, and we did.' At 5am the following Monday we were back where we started.

As spring came, the Phoney War was ending and the armies on the continent became active, the air raids more often and more heavy. Meanwhile, the armament factories, grateful for the year Chamberlain had gained, had been getting tooled-up and were going flat out. The Germans, who had been preparing for years, were winning hands-down on land, sea and in the air.

By this time, the civilian population was becoming tense as it became obvious that we were in for a long and difficult struggle. Although few ever voiced doubts about the outcome, many harboured fears of it, but all were determined to win through and buckled down to do whatever had to be done.

Life jogged along as rationing became a way of life and the names of locals appeared in the casualty lists; the war was with us for sure.

Eventually, Cyril and I, along with Henry Bird from Ind Coope, were called to report to Blackpool in June 1940.

Obviously, no one in the family was pleased about this, least of all Dorothy, who could never understand why I volunteered instead of waiting until I was called up with my age group. Perhaps it was because my father volunteered in 1914 or because some of my pals were doing so – I don't know. My father never made his opinion on this known to me. All I know is that in spite of what happened afterwards, I am still glad I did – and, I must confess, a little bit proud too.

Chapter 4

Wartime (Part 1)

On the night before I was due to report to Blackpool, I first experienced what price I had to pay as my contribution to the war. When we came to say our farewells on the doorstep of No. 78A, Dorothy returned our engagement ring and said that it was all over between us, but could give no reason why.

The next day, it was up early and off to Blackpool. I don't suppose I was good company for the two chaps I travelled with, but I kept my feelings to myself.

We reported in at our destination and were taken to 43 Alexandra Road. All the boarding houses had to take a percentage of troops among their guests. The prospect of hundreds of unattached airmen was too good to be missed, and Blackpool became a magnet for girls to spend their holiday; the result was obvious. In No. 43, several airmen went on 'night manoeuvres' before learning how to march!

On the second day, we were kitted out in a warehouse of Marks & Spencer which had been taken over. In the afternoon, we reported for inoculations which were given in the schoolroom of a little church on the corner of Alexandra Road (now replaced by a block of flats) and the sea front. Over the door of the schoolroom was an inscription: 'Suffer little children to come unto me'.

The next six weeks were spent learning foot drill and arms drill on the promenade, and attending lectures in the south pier theatre. One day we were having rifle practice, firing out to sea, just above North Pier, when a woman walking her dog ignored all the red flags and warnings and walked into the firing line. Fortunately, with the aid of much shouting and blowing of whistles, disaster was avoided. A further memory was of the day a whole host of us were marched to the Derby Baths for a swim. As we had not been pre-warned, no one had bathing trunks, the result being hundreds of nude swimmers watched by about a dozen female attendants from the balcony.

The evenings were spent at the cinema, the fun fair or – our favourite – the Tower Ballroom with Reginald Dixon at the organ.

Many Polish airmen were housed in Blackpool (as Poland was the first country to be overrun by the Germans once the war began). Because these were paid much more than English servicemen and were allowed free travel and entrance to amusements, while we had to pay, there was a good deal of ill feeling. Trouble often broke out in pubs and on the streets.

At the end of this episode we had to perform the farce of a 'Passing-out' parade – allegedly to prove our efficiency. As there was no place large enough, we had to do this on the beach, and while we tried to do smart about turns etc. in a foot of soft sand, the voice of Cyril Fletcher warned, 'If we get this right we will be in the Foreign Legion.'

Having been declared proficient, the next day saw us all being posted to various stations. Cyril Fletcher, Henry Bird and myself were in a party sent to West Raynham in Norfolk. The train journey across country took hours, calling at every village along the way. On our first night there, we were given a warm welcome by Jerry, with a raid that altered the shape of a couple of the hangars.

After a few days, thirty of us, including Henry Bird but not Cyril Fletcher, went to a place called Great Massingham, a village a few miles from the camp: just a few houses, a church, five pubs, way out in open country. We arrived to find a couple of wooden huts and a couple of tents. Already here were a first-war veteran who had re-enlisted to help the war effort, Pilot Officer Dealing, and two NCOs, Sergeant Grimes and Corporal Jones. PO Dealing was a softly spoken, grey-haired old chap who could be everyone's loving grandad. The other two had spent years swinging the lead in the RAF; with limbs trembling as a result of years of drink, and as illiterate as a brick wall, they had obviously been promoted only due to the rapid expansion caused by the war. This was a situation which I could not come to terms with, and I wondered how we could hope to win a war under such people. Thank goodness it was not long before the scene changed.

The purpose of Massingham was simple: we could operate at nights, and if we were caught by a German raid with lights on, there was nothing to be hit – only us. So No. 18 Squadron operated from here instead of Raynham, with its personnel travelling in each day. This squadron had just come back from France and was already battle-hardened, with two very good flight commanders, Squadron Leaders Sharpe and Singer, both about 5ft 6in tall and alike as twins. They equalled each other's achievements in actions and awards. One sank an enemy destroyer in the English Channel, and a couple of weeks later the other one did the same. The *Daily Mirror* had a picture of one of them, and claimed that the bomb went straight down the funnel and the ship just disappeared – or that was their story, and I suppose a bit of British propaganda.

Soon, 101 Squadron joined us. The two squadron leaders were promoted to wing commanders, taking charge of each of these squadrons, and so the rivalry continued.

I had been designated to the fire and rescue team. Apart from operating two squadrons, as we were near the East Coast we were used as an emergency landing strip for aircraft returning from missions in distress. We of course had to be in attendance while any flying was in progress, and therefore after all-night duty were often called out again during the day.

As we drew nearer to what became the Battle of Britain, our two squadrons alternated on daylight raids, while heavier squadrons from Scotland and Northern England – using Wellingtons, Hampdens and Whitleys – would come down during the day to be topped up with fuel to fly deeper into enemy territory on night operations. These were busy days and nights, but Sharpe and Singer were men everyone would give their all for – and did.

Singer once told us: 'If I had my way, I would close all the pubs and dance halls, get this job done, and then we would have something to sing and dance about.'

Sharpe led a raid on a factory, and when the intelligence reports came back it was found that a nearby treacle factory had also been hit. Cartoons appeared, drawn by some phantom, of planes dripping with treacle and such like, all bearing the caption, 'Sharpe's the word – Sharpe's the treacle', which was a well-known advertising slogan of Sharpes Caramel at the time.

We on the rescue team were having a fair amount of work, some due to enemy action and some due to raw pilots. It was not pleasant work but it had to be done, and attempting to lift a bloke heavier than myself out of a cramped fuselage, I hurt my back. The MO strapped me up and said I was to rest, so a replacement came from Raynham. After a couple of days, one of the lads operating a field telephone system got hurt and I said I could manage that job, and so I did. The thing was in a dugout which was almost permanently flooded to a depth of about a foot.

However, the place was becoming more busy and organised, and the GPO was called in to install a proper switchboard in a room of the wooden

'Ops room', which was a building shared by the Duty Pilot, Wireless Operations and the Briefing Room. This meant I moved to live in the upstairs of a large farmhouse in the village which was home to Mr and Mrs Rix and family. The work was on a three-day rota – 24 hours on duty, 24 hours doing meal relief and 24 hours off. This meant that we had plenty of spare hours, and I spent mine helping wherever hands were needed – driving tractors for the armourers, helping refuel planes and at odd times joining the crash crew. Everyone chipped in.

The extra raids which were taking place had the effect of persuading the Germans to attempt to put our aerodromes out of action, and we in Bomber Command likewise tried to keep them grounded, whilst the fighter squadrons more than had their hands full – their success is celebrated each September with Battle of Britain week. On the Sunday of the week, our planes were taking off at dusk when a flight of Jerries caught us in the act. We had planes in the air, on the runway and taxiing from dispersal, and although we lost no planes we lost a few men, including two from the rescue team.

During those few weeks, the activity was the extreme alternative to Blackpool promenade, where people were still on holiday and read about the war in the daily paper. I had written regularly to Dorothy, but had no reply, although her mother and Uncle Len had written to me.

A couple of days after this raid, I was surprised to be told that I was due for my first weekend leave. My father often used to say, 'Faint heart never won a fair lady!', and with this in mind I wrote and told Dorothy that I would be home from Friday to Monday.

I left Massingham at 8.00 am and arrived at Burton about 4pm. As I went to hand in my ticket at the barrier, there stood Dorothy. I walked her halfway home and left her on the corner of Victoria Street and Victoria Road, arranging to meet her later at 78A. I never asked why and nor was I told why she did what she did when she returned my ring, and it was only after many years of maturity that I realised Dorothy too was under pressure. Brother Lol was joining the Army, I was going away too and the civilian population were hoping that their homes would not be razed to the ground, as they had seen done in Poland and many other European countries. Although this was to be the fate of many of our cities, thankfully Burton escaped virtually unscathed.

The weekend passed all too quickly, trying to visit all relatives, and at 3.30pm on the Monday afternoon I boarded the train back to camp a much happier soul than I arrived.

Our squadrons spent the autumn and winter doing night-time raids, and we did not lose so many crews. The winter weather was atrocious, and canvas tents were erected over the engines and cockpits of the planes, which became completely buried in snow overnight and we would all help to dig them out.

The war had become a routine as far as we were concerned, and with co-operation between personnel it was possible to get more leave, although I was unlucky in the draw for Christmas 1940. On one occasion I was doing a stand-in for a lad on the crash party when a Blenheim crashed into a wood belonging to Major (retired) Birbeck and burst into flames. We were almost at the scene before it caught fire. Two of its crew of three were being pulled out by locals and we managed to get the third, although he was injured. The major was pestering about saving his trees, and as the stretcher was carried away I noticed all our volunteer assistants – and the major – had gone.

When we had dealt with the flames and were waiting for a guard to take charge of the wreckage, I learned that one of our gang had 'advised' the major to leave as there was a load of bombs on board. It wasn't true, but it cleared the area so we could do our job in peace.

There were three of us on the exchange rota: Blaze Stanway, a Welshman, Andy Berry, a true gypsy from Carlisle, and myself. Andy would sing for his beer in the village pubs, and was always prepared to stand in for Blaze and I to go into King's Lynn on Saturday evenings to the pictures. We would return with fish and chips from the next village. On one of these occasions he said: 'When we have eaten these I will show you what I have done while you have been out.' Complete with 'wellies', he took us out into the darkness and we shouted to the lads in the gun-post as we went by. Suddenly, in the pitch dark, we came upon an American Flying Fortress. There were three of them, which had been flown over by American crews in civilian clothes because at this stage they were not in the war. These were the first to come over and our crews took them over after familiarization, and their first raid was on the French port of Brest.

A further incident during that winter was when Andy, all dressed up and on his way to the pub, fell into a trench – not an ordinary trench, but one for the emptying of garbage and the Elsan toilets. He had to wash down in cold water on a very cold night, outside. For this ordeal, the MO gave him a shot of service rum; not only did he need it, he earned it.

So the autumn and winter passed, and the spring of 1941 brought us a new feature – the threat of German invasion. Little or no news of this was released, for obvious reasons, but our crews and many others were working around the clock. The main targets of our aircraft seemed to be the barges assembled on the French coast, and in moonlight raids they often caught Jerry practising loading and took a heavy toll. The German plan never got off the ground, and by now the RAF had more and better planes and was taking more control of the air.

At sea, we were still losing a lot of ships to U-boats and long-range German bombers. The Germans had two powerful ships tied up in Brest, the *Scharnhorst* and *Gneisenau*, and although they were pounded for weeks by our aircraft, they made a daring escape under cover of darkness and got home through the English Channel.

The Germans also had the powerful battleship *Bismarck*, which ventured into the North Sea and the Atlantic, where it was shadowed by a couple of our cruisers. When about half the British fleet had been mustered around it, it was attacked. The Royal Navy could not believe how much punishment the *Bismarck* took, and when it was finally disabled, it had to be sunk by torpedoes from Swordfish aircraft of the Fleet Air Arm. Later, when in the prison camp, a Lieutenant Forbes (the son of an admiral), whose ship *Prince of Wales* took part in the action, gave us a very vivid account of the battle. Forbes became a PoW in Malaya after the *Prince of Wales* was sunk by the Japanese.

As more people were now at work at Massingham, a wooden cookhouse and dining hall had been erected on a piece of land alongside the church. One lunchtime, I had just left the building when I looked up and saw that a plane about 200–300ft up was bearing swastikas. I ran back inside and shouted to the drivers of lorries parked outside to shift them out of the village. As I did this, someone opened up from one of our gun pits with small-arms fire, whereupon Jerry turned and dealt with them. It was obvious he had not seen the place until they fired, but as I stood and watched his bombs exploding, I noticed an uneven space in the string. Getting back to the aerodrome, I met Wing Commander Sharpe, who had arrived post-haste from his digs in the village, and told him what I had spotted. A search was made and the unexploded bomb was found in the entrance to the bomb store, which was just four walls of sandbags. Although Massingham grew to be a large operational aerodrome, it was never visited by Jerry again. Even our own pilots used to say that it had a natural camouflage of its own.

May came, and I was to be 21 in the June. By now I had learned a few things about planning leave. By adding a weekend pass before and after a fourteen-day leave, one could legally wangle three weeks, and if you took a chance and 'accidentally' left a couple of days between passes, you could do better still. Thus I had quite a good leave arranged.

We held a party at No. 11. I had ordered a firkin of beer (9 gallons) from the brewery, which my boss kindly paid for, and I had a good leave, although Dorothy had to work most of the time.

Unfortunately, the happiness was short-lived – and was not to return for four-and-a-half years.

Shortly after returning from leave, Stanway, Berry and myself were detailed for an overseas posting. We packed our gear and returned to West Raynham, and spent a couple of days getting 'cleared', having a dental check and inoculations. By the time my train back to West Raynham reached Sutton Bridge, I had a high temperature and was feeling as sick as the proverbial parrot. The fact that I had full kit didn't help matters, but I left this in the safe hands of the station porter. Although there was a large fighter station alongside the line (Vic Reed was stationed there at the time), it was only a village station with no facilities. I made my way across to the village pub for a drink, and the landlord spotted me straight away. Obviously well-versed in these situations, he gave me a wine glass of some sickly sweet concoction for which he wouldn't charge – and my glass of lemonade. As I sat on the train, my temperature came down, my head cleared and life became bearable again.

About halfway through my twenty-eight days' leave, the bottom appeared to drop out of the world for Dorothy and me. On my previous leave, Dorothy and I had surrendered our virginity to each other. Dorothy told me she feared that things had gone wrong. We were at our wits' end, but kept our worries to ourselves, simply because we did not know what to do and we kept hoping that we would have to do nothing.

Before we knew where we were, my leave was over and I had to report to West Kirby on Merseyside. Once again, we had parted on a sad note. The days dragged on, we drew tropical kit and waited. On the Saturday, I had news from Dorothy that the doctor had confirmed the worst of our fears and she was expecting. An interview with the officer in charge gained me leave from Monday morning until midnight on Thursday.

On the Sunday, 1,700 of us were on a huge square to assemble for church parade. As we fell in on different markers – CofE, Catholic, etc. – one lone figure was left in the middle. The flight sergeant, standing about 6ft 4in, with Glengarry green with years of service and in a crumpled heap on top of his head, bawled out like a foghorn at a little chap of

only 5ft wearing thick-rimmed glasses: 'Now Blitz, which f****** mob
do you belong to?' It transpired that he was Jewish and his name was
Blitz; the other Jews had not reported, as their church day was Saturday.

I made full speed for home on Monday, and Dorothy and I made
application for a special licence which enabled us to marry at 11am on
Thursday morning. Aunty Win and Uncle Lol acted as our witnesses
as we were married in Union Street at the Registrar's Office. We went
to No. 11 to see my Dad during his dinner hour, then to 78A to see
Dorothy's Dad during his dinner hour. I had to catch a train at 4pm to
return to West Kirby. On Friday, I showed my marriage certificate to the
RAF and filled in forms for Dorothy's allowance. By lunchtime we were
on our way to Liverpool docks, where we boarded the *Stirling Castle*,
bound for destination 'X'.

Dorothy and I didn't know that it would be four-and-a-half years
before we spent our first night together. Little did we dream how lucky we
were that we lived to see that night at all.

Postscript

Although Dorothy had never said – and I never asked – I think I know
the reason why she decided to end our engagement on the night of my
departure to join the RAF.

When the war was imminent – and you must remember that we had a
year's reprieve after the famous Munich Conference and the 'Peace in our
time' episode of Neville Chamberlain – a massive campaign was launched
on advertising hoardings, on cinema screens and in the press to try to
attract people to join the forces. Because the RAF was a new force and had
the more attractive uniform of blue with brass buttons, it was used more
extensively than the others. At the same time, a big effort was being made
to recruit girls to join the newly formed WAAF. All the media were showing
pictures of airmen with wings on their tunics and a girl on each arm, more
often than not two WAAFs. What they did not show were people living in
tents on muddy airfields miles from civilization, which was my experience.

I am as certain as I ever will be that Dorothy thought that I had fallen
for the propaganda bait. This was far from the truth, simple as I may
be. However, all is well that ends well, and here we are almost sixty
years on and still together. We have had our share of life's problems, the
same as everyone else, but any quarrels have been over in five minutes

and forgotten in six. Having said that, there are not many women who could have gone through what Dorothy has and still be as happy as she. Time has proven that I found the best one in the world – and on my own doorstep.

Wartime (Part 2)

My Experience

As we marched from the train to Gladstone Dock in Liverpool, I had been spotted by Ted Ford, who lived in Victoria Street, and he informed my parents that we had left.

We boarded the *Stirling Castle*, a luxury liner of about 30,000 tons which was in almost normal condition with very few modifications for troop-carrying. Housed in cabins of two berths, we had such facilities as a shop, hairdresser, swimming pool and concert room, just like a peacetime cruise. The civilian stewards had a 'nice little earner' going – for a small fee, they would supply early morning tea in the cabins. Much as I appreciated this, I could not enjoy it fully as my mind was back at 78A. It was to be a long, long time before I was to discover how Dorothy was managing, but I will tell you of that in the next part of this chapter.

Our first night on board was spent in Liverpool dock, where we had another new experience. Jerry decided to visit Liverpool, and an air raid while you are below deck on a ship is not a pleasant pastime. However, nothing fell around us.

Eventually we set sail only as far as the Clyde, where we were joined by other ships during the next few days. As it was August holiday weekend, the pleasure boats were doing good business and all the passengers waved and shouted good luck wishes as they passed by.

We left the Clyde late one afternoon and headed north, awakening the next morning to find ourselves part of a fair old convoy complete with naval escort. The convoy continued to head north, the weather very cold and the sea a little choppy; not our idea of an August cruise. In order to avoid enemy aircraft as much as possible, we went into the North Atlantic and then crossed towards the Canadian and American side before turning south and then back east to Sierra Leone in West Africa.

We passed these days away doing 'boat drills', PT, watching the zigzagging of the convoy (a ploy to evade submarine attack) and seeing the Royal Navy at its task. During the evenings we would walk round and round the deck or someone would organize a concert in the hall, and some good talent there was too.

Jerry didn't give us any problems. We had a few alerts, which didn't amount to anything more than the rumoured sinking of more U-boats than even Adolf boasted of having. There was one mishap when a couple of ships zigged when they should have zagged. The leader of the convoy would make a siren signal, one blast to port and two blasts to starboard. I was on deck towards the bows of the *Stirling*, and as the evasive action was so severe our bows rose and a vessel in front's stern dipped. I looked down onto it and thought we were going to have a piggyback! It was all over in seconds, but two vessels, the *Warwick Castle* and the *Windsor Castle*, were slightly damaged. They left us a little later and were taken into Halifax, Nova Scotia, for repairs, the lads having a few days holiday there.

Although America was not in the war at this time, they performed a 'Neutrality Patrol'. This was, so they said, to ensure that no vessels would be attacked in their part of the 'pond'. As there were no German or Italian vessels in this area, it was simply a diplomatic ruse to enable them to escort British convoys on this part of the journey and allow the Royal Navy to return home for further duties.

Needless to say, when the Yanks did take over our escort, we were constantly on alert and depth-charges were going off galore – it all helped relieve the boredom as nobody believed we were in any danger at this stage of the journey.

We arrived safely at Sierra Leone on the Gold Coast of West Africa, which was known as 'The white man's grave' due to malaria and other tropical diseases. We were not allowed ashore as we anchored out in the mouth of a river. We were immediately surrounded by natives in canoes, shouting 'Gissa Glasgow Bob' or 'Gissa Glasgow Tanner' (a Tanner was six pence). As the coins sank into the water, the natives would let them go quite deep before diving for them. All that could be seen was the white soles of their feet as down they went. The lads soon found this too expensive. In order to reduce the cost of the entertainment, half pennies and pennies were wrapped in silver paper, and when the natives surfaced with one of these they shouted up at us, 'You "t***er" me up Charlie!' – a sure sign that that they had been educated by members of an RAF Sunderland squadron based here, but they continued to dive as they thought the financial return worth their pastime.

After a lighter alongside had unloaded its vegetables and fruit to us, the native labourers started to fold up the sheet which had covered it.

When the task was well underway, someone threw a couple of coins in, a mad scramble started and the folding had to be done all over again. After a couple of attempts had been thwarted, the big white chief in charge decided to call it a day and fold his sheet when he got home!

The only other incident during our few days here was an air raid by some Vichy French planes operating from Dakar. They stood about as much as chance of hitting anything as they did of being the slightest use to Hitler.

From Freetown we turned south, and during this part of the journey we were told our next stop would be Cape Town, but were not told our ultimate destination. We had two or three talks on how we had to behave while ashore because of the political situation and the coloured troubles, which are still no better nearly fifty years on.

Arriving off Cape Town, we encountered the heaviest seas (known as the 'Cape Rollers') for over sixty years and were forced to lay off for 24 hours before we could get into harbour. We watched a tiny vessel pitched about and wondered how it could survive, but I think it did.

On board our vessel, we had our problems. The RAF and Royal Navy lads were down in the mess room for breakfast, all dressed in best blue ready to go ashore, when the ship gave one mighty lurch. There were men all over the place mixed up with bowls of porridge and buckets of tea – much to the amusement of the Army lads who had already been on first sitting. There were a few broken limbs, a couple of cooks were scalded and scores were seasick – but not me this time.

When we did get ashore, we were met with a really generous reception from the whites which we had been told we would. However, two pals I had made aboard and myself had decided we did not want to be taken into someone's home, as we preferred to see what we could of Cape Town. We toured the town, politely resisting many offers, and went by cable car to the top of the famous Table Mountain, from where you can see the Atlantic Ocean on one side and the Indian Ocean on the other.

On the second day we were in Woolworths, where they had one counter stacked with large oranges. For two pence they would squeeze about a pint of juice into a glass, and from a huge bowl you helped yourself to sugar. As visitors, they even refused to take our payment. As we stood enjoying our drink, two small children – one boy and one girl – came to us and said, 'Would you please be kind enough to come home with us for dinner?' By now we had become tired of refusing, and from the far side of the counter their mother smiled and beckoned us to her; we capitulated.

After introducing ourselves to each other (they were the Murray-Smith family), we made our way to their car – a huge Buick. A large basket of fruit was in the back, which we were told to help ourselves to, and we set off to see the countryside of the Cape Peninsula. As we made a start on the fruit, the two children wondered what we were doing when we began to peel the oranges; they stuck their thumbs in, tore them into two, ate the centre of each half and deposited the rest in a bag for rubbish.

We had about a three-hour tour, being constantly plied with fruit, sweets and chocolate, but each of the children put away about twice as much as we three put together. I suppose they had more practice.

We then arrived at the home of the Murray-Smith family high up in the hills overlooking Cape Town. I still haven't made up my mind whether it was a huge bungalow or a one-storey mansion – it was huge. Once inside, Mrs Murray-Smith apologized before asking if we would like to have a freshwater bath or shower, knowing that we had been some weeks aboard with only saltwater facilities. It was great to feel free from the sticky skin which the salt and special-issue soap had left us with.

The next item of conversation was food, which was the last thing on our minds, but somehow there was a decision for bacon and eggs. Mr Murray-Smith arrived home from business and went wild with delight because we were the first RAF people he had entertained (it's surprizing what small things bring pleasure to those who live in constant luxury!), and we sat down to dine.

Answering a call from Mrs Murray-Smith, a huge black cook came in with dishes of bacon and fried eggs, both stacked pyramid-style: one of eggs, one of bacon. At the insistence of our hosts, we were to take first helpings, and again our poor appetites and good manners continued to let us down. When we took an egg and a couple of pieces of bacon, Mr Murray-Smith folded his arms on the edge of the table and said, 'We are not rationed! You do it like this!' He picked up the serving slice and put a heap of eggs and a heap of bacon on each of our plates, and said, 'Help yourselves to tomatoes and fries [chips].' Once again, we failed to match the appetites of the two juniors.

During after-dinner chat, Mr Murray-Smith asked about our work back home. When I said that I worked in a brewery, the world became my oyster because he was the secretary of Lion Brewery of Cape Town. At this he took us into his cellar on a beer-tasting session, much to the delight of my two pals.

As we left the house to be taken back to our ship, there was a full moon shining through the eucalyptus trees and the evening dew forced the scent from the trees, while down below the lights of Cape Town completed an experience I will never forget. Yet the people who live with it, never even notice it.

We spent the next few days enjoying such luxury, and I could not help but keep thinking of Dorothy and the people back home. It seemed to me as if they were on a different planet, with a war to endure and less on their table in a month than was wasted from each of our meals.

Making our way back to the *Stirling Castle* on the last night of our stay, we were offered sacks of oranges to take with us from warehouses on the dockside. They were stacked here in the hope that any passing ship could take some back to England. I took a sack, and when I opened the cabin door I found my partner fast asleep, fully dressed and fully drunk, and two sacks of oranges on the floor. As plenty of fruit had been given to the ship, it was served with every meal. I can't remember what happened to it all.

Mr Murray-Smith wrote to tell Dorothy that he had seen me, and throughout the war sent her parcels of dried fruit, chocolate and butter etc. After the war, we continued to correspond and he tried hard to persuade us to go and settle in Cape Town. But I had seen at first-hand the political tension and the atrocious treatment of the black population, and it certainly was not for me or those whom I loved.

I still hold the view of South Africa which I made at the time – 'God made a beautiful country and man made a hideous mess of it.'

Off we sailed on the penultimate leg of our journey, around the Cape of Good Hope and up the Indian Ocean to Bombay.

By this time our convoy was considerably smaller, as vessels had left to destinations around the African coast. The journey was now becoming very boring; we had seen enough of flying fish and Neptune's diamonds (sulphurous deposits breaking off the ship's hull which sparkled in the darkness of the sea), which had been excitingly new to us landlubbers for a while. Boat drill had become so well practised that it was not held so often.

The only entertaining activity of note was when it was decided that the Marines were to have a firing drill with a 6in gun situated on the stern of the ship, just astern of our berths. We were all warned to stay between decks and with portholes closed. Of course, there has to be one clever dick in every class, and there was. One clown from the cabin next door had his head stuck out of the porthole to see what was going on. As the gun fired, the vessel rocked and he jumped in alarm; all he saw was stars, and he woke up with about a dozen stitches in his head. These guns were mounted as a temporary measure for the vessel to protect against attack from German 'Q' ships disguised as merchant men but actually heavily armed raiders.

We awoke one morning to find that, along with a couple of merchant vessels, we were on our own. The remainder of the convoy had gone up towards Suez, while we were a couple of days from Bombay. All this information came from crew members, as we were still officially bound for destination 'X', although it was common knowledge that we were heading for Singapore.

Being allowed a couple of days ashore in Bombay certainly showed us how the other half lived. Like in South Africa, we were warned of political tension here, as some factions in India had become tired of British rule, while others were queuing in their thousands to join the army and to fight for the British.

Going ashore we found the place full of beggars, kids chalking on your shoes and offering to clean it off at a price, snakes fighting mongooses, and everything one could imagine – and some which we couldn't dream of – offered for sale, even girls and women.

My first impression was that a recent riot had taken place; there were red stains on the pavements and walls, but I soon found out it was not blood. It was everyone chewing betel nut and spitting it out. There were teeming masses of people, everyone in dire poverty. At nights they just lay down on the pavements to sleep: dogs, people and all. Each shop had a guard to sleep in its doorway for protection. Amidst all this stood large beautiful buildings, the homes of British and Indian business people and administrators – small wonder that those who were sufficiently educated to think had decided it was time for a change.

I bought some silk whilst I was here, which I sent home to Dorothy, and with good fortune it arrived safely.

No one was sorry to leave Bombay; the odd ones who had 'joined the ladies' later wished they had not even been! As we set sail, we were at last officially told of our destination.

For us it was back to the boredom of sea travel, albeit amidst the luxury of a troopship, and off we went around the heel of India. From here we had only two freighters with us and the sea was like a mill pond, and as we neared the Straits of Malacca the sunsets and sunrises were too colourful to describe.

As we approached Singapore, we weaved our way through countless beautiful tiny islands, some too small to be inhabited. After eight weeks on the *Stirling Castle*, we thought we had arrived in paradise. Paradise it was, but not for much longer.

From the ship we were taken by bus to an RAF transit camp on the island of Singapore. The CO here was Squadron Leader Gregson, an ex-Guards officer who proved right away that he was a first-class officer; later he lived up to this first impression. After we had been fed, he gave us a short speech of welcome and wished us all well.

In this camp were a number of RAF fitters who had no squadrons to go to, so Gregson, in order to keep them occupied, had trained them up to Grenadier Guards standard. They were housed in two long bamboo huts, and over each door was a sign that read 'Gregson's X Party', and underneath in brackets 'The Fighting Fitters'. These lads were going through their paces under the charge of a sergeant, and a group of young officers who had arrived with us thought this was a huge joke – but Gregson didn't. He assembled the officers, supplied them each with a rifle taken from his squad, and proceeded to drill them. Once he had proved how useless they were, he marched them off. It was understood that he had told them that they were not on a picnic, and they returned very subdued.

We were now being sorted out for our new destinations, some to aerodromes on the island and others to various places 'up country' in Malaya. I was in a squad for a place called Kluang in the State of Johor. Destinations decided, we sat around and drinks were provided whilst we waited for our transport to our new stations. Blaze Stanway was going to Alor Setar on the north-east coast of Malaya, and Andy Berry, the third of the Massingham trio, was destined for Kota Bahru on the north-west coast. As we shook hands and said our farewells, Andy said, 'As soon as I hear gunfire I'm away home because there is nothing here which I joined up to fight for.' It was a promise he almost kept, only failing due to his own stupidity, as you will read later.

Down to the station we went. Malayan trains were wooden-seated (upholstery would soon rot and become bug-ridden), with no glass in the windows. The engines were wood-burners, which meant you were treated to sparks and smoke. As it got dark and we travelled through the jungle, we passed little bamboo huts very dimly lit by crudely made oil lamps and had our introduction to the jungle noises of the night. Interesting, but not very welcoming.

After what seemed days of journeying instead of hours, we arrived at Kluang. A sergeant and his two lorry drivers picked us up at the station, which was alongside the camp, and they took us to the dining hall about a mile inside.

Kluang was a new camp of wooden buildings with *atap* roofs (banana leaves used like thatch) and only a dozen or so people. A good meal was ready for us, and an RAF policeman sang a couple of songs at about two o'clock in the morning; he had a wonderful voice, and I always will remember how he sang 'Call, Call, Vienna Mine'. He later came round to the tables and chatted to us, and I recognized him because I saw him play once for Blackburn Rovers in a friendly at Victoria Crescent against Burton Town. I remember him because of a trick he did on the pitch which I have not seen anyone else do, before or since. I often tried, but never cracked it.

Eventually we were introduced to our billets and mosquito nets. Having no doors or windows and the camp being on the edge of the jungle, the first night with all the strange noises was looked upon with more than a little scepticism. All being dog-tired, we got off to sleep, but were later rudely awakened by a hideous wailing, and someone said, 'What the blinking heck is that?', or something like that anyway! It was the troops of the Johor Military Force chanting their prayers.

During the next weeks we were called on to do all kinds of work to make the place into what was due to be an operational station but we didn't have any planes within a hundred miles. This was to be the main petrol and bomb supply base for Malaya if Japan decided to attack us. To guard it, we didn't even have a rifle each, so up to now we could only pray that they didn't. Each day a party of us would go by road to help prepare another station on the east coast called Batu Pahat.

At Kluang we had a football pitch without one blade of grass on it, and we would have a game in the cool of the evenings. A great experience was to play against the locals, who played barefooted and could run like the wind – the only way we could win was to have a British referee.

There was nothing in the small town of Kluang except one picture house, which showed English, Malay and Chinese films on alternate nights. Two or three of us, just for the experience, went to see the Chinese version of the film *Seventh Heaven*, which we had all seen back home. It was quite an experience; the seats were only wooden benches, and the Chinese squatted on them on their haunches, smoking the most vile rubbish in their homemade pipes, spitting all over the floor and chattering away all the time like a jungle full of monkeys. An experience it was, entertainment it was not!

Whenever we wandered around the town on our off-duty days, the school teachers would try to persuade us to go in and help the kids with their English lesson. They had a hell of a time when they hijacked any of our Scotch lads. The kids all had uniforms; all wore spotless white shirts or blouses, and each school had their own bright coloured shorts and skirts. With their black hair, they all looked really cute.

Days turned into weeks, and we still had not heard from home since the day we left Liverpool. We became cheesed off with excuses for the absence of mail from loved ones, and instead of starting work one day, we all gathered at the office of the CO, who was an Australian. He said he would see what he could do about it, and in the meantime would try to organize some entertainment in the camp. What he did organize was two or three dances – I ask you, dances with no women! However, they weren't as bad as expected, because all the planters and their friends sent along their cooks, who spent all day preparing the most beautiful displays of food and fruit. In the evening, they would come along and the men would be treating the lads to drink, and the ladies and their daughters would be dancing and entertaining the boys – fresh talent on the landscape, you see.

Before this time, the planters and their ilk had not wanted to know us servicemen, but by now the prospect of war was very prominent.

Each day the Malayan newspaper dealt more and more with the threat. The whisky-swilling brass hats in Singapore were sure the Japanese would not dare to attack against our famous 18in guns. Then the papers started to put daily diagrams of Japanese ships heading towards Malaya. There was still not a sign of life from our commanders, not that they could do much anyway – we had no ships, no aircraft and nowhere near enough troops.

On the morning of 7 December 1942, a lorry-load of us were boarding to go to work at Batu Pahat as usual when Sergeant Hughes came along with a couple of rifles (between about thirty men). 'The Japs have landed up north,' he said. Our barrack comedian – a broad Geordie with a real comedian's face, raised eyebrows, black moustache, the lot – said, 'Hey up Sarge, have they come to fight us?' 'Off course they ****** well have,' replied Sergeant Hughes. 'Well you better tell them about them 18in guns on the island, 'cause we got work to do – we can't fight bloody wars an' all!'

When we arrived back at Kluang that night, the authorities had commandeered all civilian transport of every description – buses and the lot – and with native labour supervised by our RAF lads had started evacuating the drums of petrol into trains and away down to Singapore. That was a great morale-booster for a start.

A couple of days later, a plane crashed upon landing at Kluang and the pilot perished because no one knew how to get him out. A call went out for anyone who had such experience to come forward – I was the only one. The CO sent for me late that night, and gave me the task of assessing the situation and reporting back.

I found that we had a 3-ton lorry carrying twelve large extinguishers – six water and six petrol – and no rescue apparatus. There were no extinguishers or fire buckets in any of the buildings, which were all wooden, and not one hosepipe or standpipe. I reported back before 10am that day, and a signal was sent to HQ in Singapore.

A couple of days later we received a load of extinguishers and fire buckets, and I was given a couple of our lads and about twenty Tamil labourers to charge the extinguishers and fill the sand buckets. I now realized that like my father at the Dardanelles less than thirty years before, I was in a hopeless situation and the same man, Winston Churchill, was responsible.

Wartime (Part 3)

The War's Dark Days

As each day came, the Japs advanced further down the Malayan peninsula, against virtually no opposition. It was not for lack of courage on the part of our troops or our airmen; it was simply lack of numbers and equipment.

Our hopes were raised when the battleships *Prince of Wales* and *Repulse* arrived in Singapore. A few days later, I had taken what little we could in the way of extinguishers to the airfield at Batu Pahat, and as I drove along the road from the field I was stopped by a planter. You can imagine my feelings (or can you?) when he told me that these two ships, the brand new *Prince of Wales* and its companion *Repulse*, had been sunk after two days at sea and in sight of the Malayan coast. Sunk by bombs and Kamikaze pilots.

By now we were getting air raids at Kluang, although nothing serious as yet, simply because the Japs knew we had no planes and could take the place when they wanted it.

In the barrack we had a Chinese 'boot boy', Akkie, an old chap who looked about 100 years old. He worked in his bake house all night and with us during the day, snatching some sleep on his haunches in the locker room. He collected all the shoes from twenty-eight bedsides, took them out to clean and returned them all to the correct owners – much to the surprize and relief of everyone – and he did the same with the *dobie* (laundry). When Christmas came, he was invited to come back at night and have a drink with us. When you invite a Chinese, you must always expect him to bring along his friends or his family, or both – and Akkie brought his friends.

As the bottles were emptied, they were stood under the table out of the way. The party went the way of all parties, and Akkie and his mates were persuaded to climb on the tables and sing. They sang their marching songs, and our lads (and the beer) sang their version of Chinese until the trestle table collapsed on top of the empties. At this, chaos reigned and all the beds were tipped up and mosquito nets torn down; it was a complete shambles, but the lads relieved their tension.

Akkie arrived the next morning, looked around and gave a toothless grin. He held his hand to his forehead and said, 'Akkie *sakit* [sick]', turned round and disappeared. When he returned about half an hour later, he again brought his pals; one was a joiner, and they set about repairing the mosquito frames and cleaning up. They refused to have a drink as payment for their chores, and just said '*sakit*' and departed.

This was Boxing Day, and I lay on the bed wondering what Dorothy and the folks back at home were doing, because we were a day in front and it was now Christmas Day for them. After the war, I was to learn that Dorothy's lot was even worse than my own at this time.

The days of December and January saw the Japs advancing day by day. At one stage, a number of Indian troops who had seen quite a lot of action were brought out of the line for a rest and encamped in the rubber plantation. We all had in our lockers dozens of small sweat towels, which were issued to us regularly, and many blocks of soap, which were given to us by the Chinese staff in the Naafi in lieu of change (I think they had a good fiddle going on with this).

Anyway, we gave some of these to the Indian troops and invited them to use our showers (always only cold water). Their major was quite pleased by this and invited some of us to his tent for a meal. It was curried chicken and rice. The Indians carried live chickens; they would ring its neck and start plucking it before it was properly dead, and in less than no time it would be chopped up and frying.

The Japs were by now closing in on us and paid us a little more attention. On one occasion, they hit a stack of petrol drums and we were powerless to do anything about it. We got caught out one day without warning, and I made my way to the so-called fire-wagon and could see smoke coming from the direction of the officers' block. No one else was around, so I made my way over to it on the opposite side of the camp to discover an army gun-limber on fire. Only the tyres were ablaze, and I was able to put them out. When it was all quiet and the rabbits came out of their holes, the CO sent for me and tore a strip off me for putting myself in danger as the limber was loaded with shells. I said, 'Had it continued to burn, it would have blown you lot to Singapore.' While the CO was having a go at me, the captain whose limber it was came in and tried to argue my case. This only made the CO worse, and I got fed up so I asked if I could have a leave pass and a travel warrant to take me back to England, where even civilians were trying to win the war. At this he shouted, 'Get out of my office!', which I did, and never went in again actually. I suppose he was some clerk or such from the RAAF (Royal Australian Air Force). The attitude of this officer, whose name I don't think I ever knew, was one which unfortunately was to be encountered far too often in the months to come. He held the rank of flight lieutenant.

On Christmas Day, Air Chief Marshal Brooke-Popham, who was CinC Far East Command, issued his order of the day to his troops. The final paragraph read: 'I know the limited resources which fate has set at our disposal but I trust you will go forward to earn undying fame for yourselves and your squadrons.' An orderly-room clerk, detailed to post copies in vantage points around the camp, got 'jankers' (military slang for a punishment) for posting them inside toilet doors. Brooke-Popham was one of the first to be recalled to safety from Singapore.

Each day the task of ferrying drums of petrol to the railway for transit continued, but as the Japs got closer, the Chinese and Malays of the civilian forces just melted away. They seemed to know better than we did just what the situation was.

Eventually, one day late in January, the order came for Kluang to be evacuated and to withdraw to Singapore. I was one of those due to stay behind to help in a demolition job and set fire to the buildings. Even this plan failed, as we had to move out in a hurry as the Japs were already here.

I arrived with a small party back at the transit camp, wearing a gym shoe on one foot due to an ingrowing toe nail. Along came Squadron Leader Gregson to do his usual inspection, and he dispatched me to see the MO. In a couple of days I had my shoe on again.

Singapore was now getting plenty of rough treatment, being shelled from Malaya and bombed at will. A few Hurricanes had arrived in crates, and these were assembled on the roadside and took-off from the roadway. They had no effect at all. We were called upon to go out and unblock roads covered with debris, and load material for the docks. On one such occasion, I was trying to take one of the 60ft articulators loaded with RAF spares to the docks via the Chinese quarter. It was the first time I had handled anything like this, and although it was strictly a job for better drivers, it just had to be done. A couple of lads were guiding me round a tight corner, and as always, in this district there was a lot of noise. When eventually we got clear and one of the lads rejoined me, he said we had crushed an old Chinese chap against the wall, but the local policeman told us to carry on and get out of the way – life was even cheaper than ever now that a war was on.

The famous 18in guns were now firing blindly into the jungle of Malaya, having had the concrete turrets removed to enable this. It had always been a myth that Singapore would have to be taken from the sea because no enemy force could penetrate the jungle: one more example of the inefficiency of people who only interested themselves in the affairs of the Raffles Hotel. Small wonder that troops would march along singing, 'We are marching on to Raffles Square, Raffles Square, where they don't know sugar from shit!'

One day I was in a party of seventy-five and we were sent into Seletar airbase, which had been evacuated. Seletar was at this time the world's largest airbase. A large amount of spirits had been left in the Naafi Stores cellar, and it had to be destroyed or salvaged to prevent the possibility of hordes of drunken Japs rampaging through the island. We went in with three lorries, travelling at speed and a distance from each other. We loaded them up and left without incident. The second trip was different; as soon as we went in, they started to shell the place. We managed to load up again, then smashed scores of bottles of whisky, set the place on fire and made for safety again.

When we arrived back at the transit camp, we were met by Squadron Leader Gregson again and he told us to stay on the lorries and head for Tengah air base, which was the last one open. There we boarded three Dutch aircraft, twenty-five on each, and flew off to Palembang in Sumatra.

Gregson and his 'Fighting Fitters' did some good work during the fighting in Singapore, which fell a couple of days after we left.

We were taken from the aerodrome of Palembang into the town and to an empty school. There was not one item of furniture of any description in the place, we had left all our kit behind and had not eaten for hours, and it was now mid-evening. All the lads had a couple of bottles of some kind of spirits which they had collected. Not being interested in booze, I had acquired a haversack full of Horlicks tablets, which proved to be more than useful during the next few weeks.

We saw some Dutch officers and asked them for help, and eventually a mobile kitchen from the Dutch barracks came along with a hot meal for us, but first they had to send back to their base for eating utensils for us, and good aluminium gear it was. The food was first-class, and as we sat eating on the tiled floor of the school, a lorry arrived loaded with mattresses. With our immediate needs supplied, we decided to get some sleep and wait to see what the next day brought.

During the night, arrangements had been made for the Dutch to feed us. That issue settled, the next item was a change of clothing – essential in the tropics obviously. We made individual efforts to acquire this however we could. The result was a mixture of khaki, green or white, and we looked nothing at all like an efficient mob.

Each day we would wander around the town and make our way in odds and sods up to the RAF at the aerodrome about 4 miles away to try and get hold of some money. We didn't have any luck because we did not belong to anyone – neither did we have any pay books.

About half a dozen of us were at the aerodrome after money one day, when our luck changed, but not for the better. The siren went, and not only was the place bombed and strafed, but paratroopers dropped; this was a new ordeal for us because we didn't even know the Japs had any paras.

Fortunately, the visitors landed in the trees on the far side from us, but the din and confusion was unbelievable. Some Army officer said to us: 'Take your rifles and join my troop over there.' When we told him we had no such thing, he told us to '**** off out of the place'. This was a fairly good idea, but was easier said than done. Apart from Jap fighters strafing the place, the Dutch Ambonese troops were trigger happy and had a pop at anything that moved. Bit by bit, about six of us found our way into some bushes and eventually found a road. We walked alongside the road, keeping in the cover of the trees, and after a long trek made our way out – still with no money. The town of Palembang was rife with rumours as we made our way back to the little school, only for some of the other lads to tell us it served us right for being money-grabbers! Anyway, our evening meal arrived, so we settled down for the night, but there was a lot of activity on the streets all night.

We got little or no sleep, and were paid several visits by various Dutch military personnel and police, all with conflicting stories and useless advice. I had heard many tales of 'Fred Karno's Army'[1] – a music hall gang – but now I was sure I was in his air force!

Just after dawn, along came the Dutch mobile cookhouse with coffee and bread rolls with jam, and as we sat eating, at last came an instruction which was alleged to have come from 'a high-ranking British officer'. We were to

---

[1] Frederick John Westcott (1866–1941), best known by his stage name Fred Karno, was a theatre impresario of the British music hall. 'Fred Karno's Army' included Charlie Chaplin and Stan Laurel.

go to the railway station and get onto a train to go to 'some other place', wherever that may be.

Lorries came and took us to a marshalling yard, where we met some British Army and RAF officers who knew no more about what was happening than we did. Anyhow, we boarded a train and after endless hours of journeying we found ourselves on the banks of a river. A couple of ferryboats were to take us across, and on the way we were attacked by Jap fighter planes. The only defence we had came from an RAF officer who stood and fired back with a Tommy gun. As the boat was packed tight with people, many got hit, but we made it to the opposite bank, where we boarded another train. Eventually, late at night, we arrived at a place called Lahat, and here again confusion was the order of the day (or night).

Because we had been sent to the wrong place, we were given a hot meal of stew and bread, a drink of coffee, and were loaded onto flat bogies. It appeared that we had to retrace our journey to the railhead before the Japs cut us off, as we had gone into a cul-de-sac in central Sumatra. Only wearing shirts and shorts, and lying on the hard-boarded floor of loose-coupled wagons all through a cold night, we arrived at the small port of Costhaven completely shattered.

All the oil wells there were being blown up, and the pillars of smoke rose into the sky. It seemed that the whole world was on fire. After all sorts of people had done a lot of shouting and arm waving, we were put on board a Chinese junk, which I wouldn't have trusted to cross the Trent. To be fair, the Chinese crew did their best for us and gave us rice balls and tea (no sugar or milk), and we set off for Java. By now we were so exhausted we just curled up and slept, amid cockroaches, mice and all.

It was only a short journey across the narrow straits – but a journey which could only be described as from hell to heaven. We entered a large tranquil lagoon, with silver sandy beach, white surf, blue seas and edged with palm trees. It was a scene straight from a film set. Once ashore, we were amazed to find a train was waiting for us only about 50 yards from the beach, which was apparently a haven for the wealthy Dutch. Before we boarded the train, we were served with drinks and snacks by a group of Dutch and Indonesian ladies. I will always remember one of the Indonesian girls – a real beauty with long black hair and dressed in pale blue, just to complement the film set. (Don't worry, I have often told Dorothy of this flirting moment or two!)

Anyway, off we went and eventually reached Batavia (now Jakarta). Here we found lots of troops, mostly RAF, who had arrived too late to get into Singapore and had been disembarked here, unarmed, the ships sailing away empty. Troops were housed mainly at schools and evacuated convents, and once again we were back from the sublime to the chaotic. It was here that I saw Aircraftsman Blitz, who had made his mark on the church parade at West Kirby. He was in khaki drill, complete with pith helmet, and riding a huge cross-framed bicycle built for a 6ft 6in Dutchman; not able to reach the saddle, he was just able to straddle the cross-frame. Flying along the main highway, causing amusement for all – especially the natives – he was hardly the desired image of a British serviceman abroad.

After a couple of days hanging around, I was one of a small group dispatched to a Dutch airfield at Kalidjati. Once again, there was nothing for us to do. We were housed in what I believe had been the homes of Javanese troops and their families who had now been evacuated. With no news from home since I left England, I was more and more concerned about Dorothy, and now – late February – was the time she was due to have our firstborn. I don't know if this took my mind off the war or the war took my mind off Dorothy. Actually, I think I was just about out of my mind altogether. Whichever way it was, I became fully occupied on 1 March 1942 – it was Sunday and Dorothy's birthday, and I imagined I was invited to her party.

A group of us were awakened at around 3am and taken onto the airfield in the pitch dark. We were informed that the Japs had made a landing on the coast, the Dutch troops had to go to 'fulfil their arrangements' and we were to replace them.

It transpired that eighteen of us were to take over six gun-posts which had already been evacuated by scores of Dutch-officered Javanese troops. Thus we formed teams of three. Being an LAC (Leading Aircraftman), I was to take charge of two lads who had just come off the boat and we were to man one of these posts. Upon being directed to our post, we had to find our way into it through masses of barbed wire in pitch darkness. Once in, we could do little but grope around until dawn broke. A telephone rang, and guided by the sound I located it and an RAF sergeant answered. He told me to keep alert and expect trouble, and promised to send us some food later – we are still waiting for that!

Dawn came, the food didn't, and when I saw the crew of a Royal Artillery (RA) Bofors gun packing up from a nearby site, I sent one of the two lads across the field to get some news (the phone was now dead) and something to eat if possible. After some time, the lad, whose name I have never known, came back and said that almost everyone had left and the remainder were on their way out. At this I decided that as there was no easy way out of this barbed wire, and as our position was hopeless, we would get out now. It was no good sacrificing our three lives for a useless cause which our officers and others had already abandoned. I stripped breach blocks from the guns to disable them, and the lads hurled them into a nearby brook and bracken. We then took a Lewis gun, some ammunition and a couple of rifles, and made our way back across the airfield to get a lift out.

Halfway across the field, we met a carload of air crew lads who asked, 'Where are you going?' When I said 'To headquarters', I was told that the only people in there were Japanese. As we hung on to the running boards of the car, heading back where we had come from, all hell broke loose. The Japs were deadly in their use of mortars, but I think the Gods gave Dorothy and I a birthday present as we arrived back safely and sought refuge in a ditch.

From this position, we watched as a couple of tanks and lorry loads of Japs burst onto the airfield. Our luck held, as they took the route along the airstrip which was away from us. A junior officer from the RA came to us and directed us towards some lorries which he was trying to get away. I was put aboard a petrol bowser with the optimistic supposition that my Lewis would protect it as we passed the area occupied by the Japs. We left one at a time to avoid exposing a whole group of vehicles to one ambush; our vehicle got through safely and we made our way to Bandoeng.

The events at Kalidjati were a mystery to historians after the war, due solely to the lack of survivors. Of our eighteen, only two survive today. All those caught on the aerodrome were shot or bayoneted as they surrendered, and a further two or three died in captivity. I was the first (in 1988) to give an account of the scene, with the aid of maps provided by the Java FEPOW (Far East Prisoners of War) Club. The story of surrendering men being bayoneted was told by PoWs taken back there by Japs to tidy up the aerodrome.

Thus was spent Dorothy's birthday.

After a couple of days in Bandoeng, I was on a convoy heading for the coast to await some ships which were allegedly to collect us. The AOC East Java was in charge, one Air Commodore Staton (from Staton Gypsum at Tutbury), an ex-Guild Street School boy like myself. We halted on a hillside and I lay under a tree completely exhausted, waking the next morning to find that it had poured with rain during most of the night. I was just as saturated as those who had stayed awake.

On Sunday 8 March, some Dutch officers and officials arrived to tell us that they had capitulated in order to save their homes from being destroyed, and that we must also surrender as they had told the Japs where we were. The hopes which the Dutch held that they would carry on as usual under the Japanese were soon shattered when they found themselves in captivity alongside us. While we were waiting for orders from the Japs where to proceed, a large Dutch security van full of gulden coins (each worth more in metal than their face value) was rolled over the cliff face and lay hidden in the jungle to be retrieved after the war. In 1988, on holiday at Paignton in Devon, Dorothy and I met a young Dutch couple in the hotel. When I related this incident, they talked excitedly to each other in Dutch, and then told us that the man had been told about this by his stepfather, who had taken part in pushing the truck over the cliff.

Eventually we were rounded up, and as I was covered in septic sores caused by sweat, sludge and tramping around in the jungle undergrowth, I was sent to a hospital in Bandoeng, wondering what the future had in store and what was happening to Dorothy and our families back in Burton – and when I would see them again. Never did I doubt that I would see them again, although sometimes my confidence was shaken more than a little.

The Darkest Days Before the Dawn

I don't know where the main body of our convoy was directed to, but we arrived at St Vincentius in Bandoeng. Seated on the steps in front of this place were two Australian MOs sorting out the various types of complaint. One of these was a huge fellow, who I later knew as Captain McMara. As I was being examined by his counterpart, McMara was interviewing a young lad who had contracted VD and was crying his heart out. He got no sympathy from McMara, who bawled out, 'Was she black or white? And I want no bloody fairy stories.'

At this stage the Japs had not got organized, and the hospital functioned normally. The senior MO was Lieutenant Colonel Dunlop (later known as 'Weary'), and one of his achievements here was to save the life of Bill Griffiths, who lost both his hands and his eyes while removing ammunition which had been booby-trapped. (Dorothy and I met him at Stratford-upon-Avon last year.)

Many of us were soon restored to health and wondered when this life of idleness and comfort would come to an end. Come to an end it did when all those who were able to walk were marched off to discover life at the other end of the scale.

The Jap guards were trying to hurry us along, but we had to take our time due to those who were not really fit enough to march; a few unpleasant encounters took place as the guards lost their tempers.

We arrived at a native gaol with the name of Slandopovoedingogesticht. The cell blocks stood around a small muddy compound, and we were herded into these until there was insufficient room to lie down on the bare tiled floor. This place was simply hell. The native prisoners, whom we were told were all murderers, were in the next compound and would pass through our compound on their way to work. They walked in single file, all chained together, and the last one would have a keg of water on his shoulder.

There was nothing to do, the food was rice only, and it was here we had our heads shaved. The guards were hostile, and scores of lads got beaten up for no apparent reason. Fortunately, our stay in this place did not last long, as without warning, we were told to pack up (if you had anything to pack – I didn't) and were marched to the railway station. It was a long march in tropical heat, and I was wearing a pair of sailors' blue bell-bottom UK-issue trousers.

At the station we were allowed to refill our bottles with water before boarding the wooden-seated train. We were on that train for hours on our way to Batavia. I had been fortunate enough to get a seat, and while others were speculating as to where we were and where we were going, I couldn't care less. All I could think of was, 'What was Dorothy doing?', 'Was the baby born yet?' and 'When will we see each other again?'

Arriving in Batavia, we had another short march to another native gaol called Boei Glodok. After endless headcounts and recounts, we were let inside. This place was more spacious than the previous one, and by the time we had been allocated to our cells, those already in camp supplied a meal of rice and weak but warm soup and some tea. After our previous rice-only meals and a long, hot journey, we thought we were at the Ritz.

The Japs were now getting their act together and working parties were organized. Most went to work on the aerodrome, some in a field outside the gaol walls to grow food and others each day to a garage.

All vehicles had been confiscated and parked outside the town. They were fetched in about six at a time to this garage, which was soon christened 'One stop'. The vehicle bodies were destroyed, but the Japs wanted the engines, radiators and front grills. Each gang of chaps was given a bunch of different coloured labels and the job of dismantling these engines and wiring the labels on to the components.

It was soon noticed by the 'stupid Ingeris soldiers' that the clever Nippon guards knew sweet Fanny Adams about car engines, and that the *Sloko* (sergeant) who did, only visited on Tuesday and Friday. Alongside this garage ran a river, and what with a few irreplaceable parts falling in there and a few more exchanged between gangs, we were able to show our gratitude to Japan by presenting them with the biggest jigsaw puzzle in the world. Our only fears were: being caught at it, being at the other end to rebuild them or the river being dammed before we left. Fortunately, none of these things happened.

In order to save time each night at '*Tenko*' (roll-call), it was decided to do it cell by cell. To facilitate this, we had to learn to count in Japanese and were only given a couple of hours to do so. It was decided that the people who stood either side of the doorway should know the total, so whichever way round they decided we should count we were safe. Each one round the room made a noise and the last one called the total. This was a success, and as we all learned the lingo it kept us out of trouble. Then one day the Nippon guard – 'he know Ingeris soldier was no good soldier' – with a big grin on his face and a big stick in his hand, decided to start in the middle. It was too late, we knew the answer. Winning these simple battles made life a little brighter, but when we lost one it was a tragedy.

A couple of air-crew lads,[1] whilst working on the aerodrome, had weighed up the situation and decided to make a break by stealing a plane and heading for Australia. They got to the airfield but could only get one engine started, and so were caught. This meant hours of standing out on roll-call for all of us. Our officers were given a rough time for days, and the chaps who slept on either side of the two were taken away by the *Kenpeitai* (Japanese military police). These six were never seen again, and meanwhile our rations were halved for quite a long period.

Later, when things returned to normal, there was a concert party formed, which gave a show each Saturday night, with the Japs allowing them to collect a few props and costumes from a theatre in town. On one occasion, a lad who had dressed up as an ice-cream sales girl – complete with black stockings, etc. – and walked among the lads was stripped by the guards, who thought a girl had been smuggled into the camp! With about a thousand blokes, she'd have been so lucky! It was at this camp where a stork nested in a tree – she had no luck either. The stay in this camp was the best of our captive days, although it was not all honey.

From one working party, one of the native troops cleared off and we were in trouble again. The officer in charge of the party was Squadron Leader Wigram, who claimed to be the oldest serviceman in the Far East. He was knocked about terribly and put into solitary confinement on starvation rations. Someone passed some food into him, but the Japs got to know. It was generally thought that a Dutchman gave them a tip-off. This had us all standing out on the field again until someone owned up. The Jap commandant said: "All men will stand – one month, two months, rain or shine, no sleep, no sit down, no sleep, all standing'. After a while, an RAF officer, in order to release everyone else, owned up, although he was not the guilty person. He was beaten up and given

---

[1] In September 1989, while on holiday at Pontins, I learned that these men survived punishment, and the two escapees were living in Australia.

the same treatment as Wigram. Sometime later (weeks rather than days, I can't remember exactly), the Oriental mind baffled us again. Without warning, both of these officers were taken out of camp, and of course we feared the worst, but thank heavens without cause. They were actually taken to the quarters of the Jap commandant and given a slap-up feed. We were all called on parade again, and the Jap commandant told us how brave these two men were, but if anyone else escaped all men in the camp would be punished – not only those who made the attempt.

It was in this camp I met the only Burtonian I ever came across in captivity; Reg Soloman, who still lives in Horninglow Street. His brother is 'Solly', of St Andrew's Drive.

By now we were accepting as normal the very poor washing facilities and complete lack of toilet facilities. I won't go into the sordid details, only to say that the ingenuity of people to overcome these situations were out of this world. It was thanks to the ability of a few and their hard work, coupled with the co-operation of everyone, that so few epidemics occurred. Inevitably some did break out, and with a complete lack of medical supplies in some camps these were disastrous, particularly later on.

All MOs had acquired what supplies they could, smuggled them into the camps. Such stock was used with great skill and care, and many people alive today owe it to the MOs and orderlies who performed almost miracles under atrocious conditions.

After Boei Glodok, I moved to several camps. I cannot remember the names of all of them, or in which order they came, but I will tell you what I can of instances I recall, if not exactly where they happened.

I do know that the next camp I went to was Tjamati. This was a huge barracks with Australian, Dutch, Ambonese,[2] Javanese and British POWs.

Here again we seemed to have time on our hands, and that was the last thing we wanted. I would sit all day on my haunches, with only home and Dorothy to think of. Unlike the majority of people, who belonged to a unit or regiment, I had from the time I left Kluang been separated from my pals and was a loner.

One day, an RAF bloke came and sat down beside me. 'How are you doing, chummy?' he said. Even now, after all these years, I get uptight when I recall that moment. If things have got on top of me at times, I have

---

[2] Ambonese: people of Ambon Island, part of the Maluku Islands of Indonesia. The island was captured from Allied forces by the Japanese in 1942.

remembered how those five kind words saved my life, and have pulled my socks up and got on with it.

The complete stranger who came to me was to become my pal for life, indeed *the* pal of life. He would come and talk two or three times a day, and persuade me to have a walk round and round the camp. He was Jack Brown, a medical orderly. I was introduced to his pal, another medical orderly, Tom Clarke. Jack came from Oxford – he was a superintendent in a psychiatric hospital – while Tom was a reporter for a newspaper in Barrow-in-Furness. An odd couple, but a wonderful pair. Although I was not aware of it at the time, I later realised that they saved me from fading away and dying of what became known as melancholia – a broken heart, it's often called. This was in the early days of our internment, and Jack's words rang in my ears whenever the going got tough, although we were not often in the same camps. During the next three-and-a-half years, I knew and saw many lads who died simply because they lost hope, just as I would have done if Jack Brown had not taken me under his wing, as he also did for many others.

It was in this camp that someone produced, of all things, a football. A league was started between nationalities, and I played for England along with Jack. Wales were top of this league by miles, as they had several Cardiff City players, including a brilliant goalkeeper named Tobin. I don't know which gave out first, the life of the ball or the strength of the players.

The CO of the British and Australian sector of this camp was the one and only Lieutenant Colonel 'Weary' Dunlop. 'Weary' stood well over 6ft tall, and was always around among the troops. If there was any trouble with the Jap guards, he was on the spot to intervene. He was absolutely fearless, and his actions often got him into trouble, but his consistent refusal to be browbeaten eventually won him some respect from our hosts. Due to 'Weary', the hostility of the guards whilst we were in this camp was greatly curtailed.

Another noteworthy character surfaced on the scene at this camp, one Colonel Laurens van der Post, who it turned out was an Intelligence Officer. Many books have been written of him and by him since the war. He has also done much broadcasting on radio and television. A great friend and guru of Prince Charles, he became godfather to Prince William. It appears that throughout his internment, he remained in touch with the outside world through his contacts with mainly Chinese associates.

It was because Van der Post was able to supply a limited amount of paper that Tom Clarke, with help from others, was able to produce a camp newspaper. Aptly titled *Mark Time*, a few copies were produced, and after being passed around were raffled off. As these appeared in the early days of captivity, very few survived. In camp was a caricature artist from a newspaper (I believe Australian[3]), and in issue one, quite rightly, was a life-like one of 'Weary' Dunlop. After the war, I was given one of these copies, which could well be the only surviving one. I passed it on to the RAF Museum at Hendon to be saved for posterity.

By now it was Christmas 1942, and with us was a Welsh artillery captain who was a spitting image of 'Old Bill' of *The Better 'ole* fame: a round red face, full bristly moustache and always smiling. As his name was Captain Christmas, a life-like caricature of him appeared on a special Christmas issue of the camp paper, with the caption 'A Merry Christmas' – typical of Tom Clarke's journalistic art.

This was our first Christmas in captivity, and the atmosphere in the camp was unreal to say the least. Everyone was pretending to be happy, but wasn't. Everyone wanted to be alone with their thoughts of home, but everyone else was determined not to let them be so. I suppose we could best be described as a crowd of broken-hearted clowns. What is for sure is that Christmas Day ended early in 1942, as everyone got their heads down early in order to have those minutes of solitude. Being seven or eight hours ahead of European time, I lay down and tried to picture those at home sitting down to dinner and wondering what they were doing. One thing the Japs did always do was to honour our Christmas Day and give us a day off work.

From this time on, things began to get much more unpleasant and the guards more touchy. There were the odd radios around occasionally, and we were lead to believe, although we had no confirmation that it was fact, that the Japanese progress had been stemmed in the Pacific.

We were now constantly moved from camp to camp, and drafts of men were being sent away from Java. (We later discovered they went to Japan and the remote islands of Ambon and Harokoe. The latter two were horrific, and lads died in their hundreds of disease and starvation.)

One camp I went to was Tandjong Priok. This had been a camp for natives working on the docks of Batavia. The buildings were open-fronted and could best be described as long back-to-back verandas partitioned into

---

[3] Sid Scales: born 1916 in Ashburton, New Zealand, died 2003 in Motueka. He was a New Zealand cartoonist.

sections. The sanitation and water supply were almost non-existent, and the camp's only assets were that it had a large open field space and was on the coast, so we were allowed to bathe there after work. Although the beach was good, the sea was home to large jellyfish which could (and did) sting like hell – the lads swore blind that the Japs imported them just to make life unpleasant for us.

Here we worked long, hard and monotonous hours on the docks. We would spend days unloading drums of oil and petrol from ships into the sheds. Next we would load them onto railway trucks, and they would be taken to a place we christened 'Coconut Grove' to be unloaded and stored.

As we always seemed to be in a hurry to clear the ships for the Japs, clear the shed for another load or load the train faster than the last one, the guards were always hostile and we had lots of nasty incidents – but a few laughs too.

On one occasion, a German 'Q' ship came in to refuel. It was good to see the German crew in their smart white uniforms, and 'Johnny Jap', sword getting tangled up in his jack-boots, trying to walk with them. It was even better when, after the Germans had given cigarettes to some of our lads, the Nips tried to confiscate them. The Germans came back, arguments turned to blows and Japs went flying everywhere. It would have been fatal for us to make a move to even get out of the way, but we had a few minutes' enjoyable excitement. The aftermath was that we had to work a couple of hours longer and tread very carefully for some days afterwards.

Someone had a bright idea one day to lay a plank of wood that he found with nails in, on the shed floor in the dark. The hope was that drums rolling over it would puncture, leak, and up would go the whole lot. The Japs discovered a pool of petrol almost as soon as it started, and although we got away with claiming it was an accident, it was made clear to us that if a fire started in future, we would have to deal with it. We didn't reckon that was a fair deal, so never tried that trick again.

On another occasion, after we had worked all day, loading train after train with oil drums, we were given our evening meal of rice and soup and told we had to work all night. The guards were changed and the officer in charge, dressed in an immaculate white uniform, stood in the doorway all night long. As each train was filled, he would say 'satu lagi' (Japanese for 'one more'). The lads were all cheesed off and were calling him all sorts of slant-eyed yellow parentless names under the sun. As a new guard came out on the following morning, he pulled a piece of chalk out of his pocket and wrote on the side of the last truck, 'Thank you, you have done your best' in perfect English. He just walked away, and we just stood and stared – one to 'Johnny Jap' this time.

We had just settled down for the night after one such day, lying on a *tika* mat (like a beach mat), when the concrete floor started to bend. People started getting up and running about, and someone was shouting, 'Get out in the open'. This was a new experience – an earthquake. Fortunately, it was not severe and only lasted a few minutes, but all the same if was not very pleasant.

It was while in this camp that the Japs decided some propaganda was due in order to let the world know how well we were being looked after. They took some chaps outside to a local theatre and fetched costumes, scenery, piano, musical instruments etc., so that we could have a good concert.

We had in our midst one Clepham Bell, a Shakespearean actor who had put on small plays, and he was charged with organizing one such. As always among servicemen, there was always plenty of talent and it was decided to perform The White Horse Inn. The 'in camp' rumour around this time was that for the first time the RAF had gained control of the skies in North Africa, and this had enabled Monty's forces to gain control there. Thus the stage was set, and the backcloth was a huge 'V' in Air Force blue. Japanese officers were in the front row seats, and the cameras had a field day. We all enjoyed the concert, although we didn't know whether the news had been fact or just a morale-boosting rumour put about by our own officers.

Clepham Bell was later taken away to do propaganda broadcasting, and the news was that he was shot for refusing to do so. Knowing him, I could believe that; he was never seen again anyway.

It was whilst in this camp that a questionnaire went around asking what our jobs were. These had been done before when our hosts were looking for people for drafts, so now everyone was attempting to be as useless as possible – I was a beer taster in a brewery. Among a host of labourers, dog catchers, etc., the prize this time went to a couple of Aussies. One was a cat burglar, the other a snow-dropper (in Australia?). Upon explaining what a cat burglar did for a living, he was immediately put in a cell; he did no work and was well-fed for quite a while – funny minds these Japs had.

Another camp I recall was the notorious Cycle Camp, so called because it was the home of a Dutch Regiment of cycling troops. The Japanese commandant was to become a legend for his eccentricity – the one and only Lieutenant Soni. A real nasty piece of work was Soni, and I had two spells in there, but thankfully fairly short spells.

'Sonny Boy', as he became known, marched around the camp with his arms swinging almost shoulder high, and his guards had to do likewise in order to show the 'Ingeris' and 'Mexicanos' what good soldiers Nippon soldiers were. He didn't like it, however, when he caught prisoners taking the Mickey by doing likewise.

The guards, like Soni, were always looking for trouble, and someone was always getting a beating for no reason at all. Day and night, the place was sheer hell.

From this camp, a working party used to go to a Jap marines barracks, cutting grass etc. This was a good party to get on, as many marines and all their officers had been to England or America for training, and they would always find some extra food and fruit for us. Soni was aware of this, and when the party returned, they would be searched to ensure that no food was brought back into camp and would be kept standing on parade for anything over an hour before being allowed in.

It was my unhappy experience on one of my stays here to sleep alongside a Canadian sergeant pilot who had a radio concealed in a water bottle. Had it been discovered, the consequences for him and those close to him would have been summary. I don't hide the fact that I was pleased when we became parted.

We were lined up for '*Tenko*' one evening alongside a large cage of monkeys which Soni kept, when there was one unholy clatter. One of the monkeys had pushed over a large piece of boarding, causing a loud bang and a huge cloud of dust. We stood facing it and could see what happened, but poor old Soni soiled his underpants. He went crazy, storming into the cage and cutting down all the swings with his sword, but was not fast enough to catch his monkeys. Then he turned his wrath on us because we had all laughed at him, and consequently we stood there until the early hours of the following morning.

On my first visit to Cycle-Camp, I was reunited with Jack Brown, and when he was selected to be on a draft, he pulled some strings in order that I went with him.

This transpired to be a draft of 1,015 men to return to Boei Glodok: 1,000 to make string and fifteen for administration and hygiene duties. I was to work with Jack and a couple of others in the so-called sick bay. There were four doctors in camp: two RAF, Dawson and Morgan; one Royal Navy, Lieutenant Wyatt from HMS *Exeter*; and one Royal Artillery, named Goronwy, a Welshman. We also had a dentist, Flight Lieutenant Frank Graham.

One of the guards came in to complain of not being able to sleep, and was told to call when he came off duty and he would be given some medicine. He insisted on having some here and now. and began to get very hostile, so he was given his 'dope'. The outcome was that he fell asleep and tumbled out of his sentry box, which was on top of a 15ft wall. Luckily for us, the Jap medical sergeant was on good terms with our MOs because Dawson had learned to speak Japanese. The guard, for his trouble, was beaten up and sent to a hard labour camp.

When the lad who was dental orderly was sent on a draft, I took on his duties and became assistant to Flight Lieutenant Graham. One day Graham was down sick and a guard who was a regular patient came in complaining of toothache. This was because he would not have the tooth extracted, but he would not accept that I was only the assistant and demanded that I now treat him in Graham's absence. We got to the situation where he became hostile and threatening, then one of the orderlies, Ron Meredith, said, 'Somebody is going to get hurt, Jim, and I suggest it be him rather than you – I'll help you.' Realizing these were the best odds on offer, I decided to have a go myself as I had seen it done half a dozen times anyway. It was a matter of grinding out a soft dressing, putting in some oil of cloves and replacing a soft filling. With the aid of Meredith and God's guiding hand, we got away with it successfully. The next day, the guard returned with tablets of soap, sugar and bananas, which we all decided was not a bad alternative to the butt-end of a rifle. He was my first – and only – dental patient.

It was while in this camp, when I was lying sick with fever, that Graham came to see me, as he did a couple of times each day. He squatted down beside me as I lay on the floor and said: 'I have two or three letters for you, Jim. Only a few came into camp, and you are one of the lucky ones.' Thus I learned that my son David was born; it was now March 1944 and he was over 2 years old.

After the war, Frank Graham wrote to me every Christmas until his death a few years ago. Dorothy and I called on him at his home in Marple, Cheshire, when we were out driving one Sunday, and he was pleased to see us.

We had spent Christmas 1943 in Glodok, and again it was made a day's holiday by the Japs. In one of the alleyways was a large wooden vessel shaped like half a cask, which was always full of water. The lads were dragging the officers along and chucking them in. The Jap commandant laughed himself silly and thought this great fun, joining in by fetching his guards along one at a time for the same treatment! We thought that was ever better fun because they were fully clothed – long johns, puttees, boots, the lot.

We had one hairy experience when we were awoken to find the camp full of *Kenpeitai* and us confined to our cells. The search was on for a radio. Everything was turned over, even the roof spaces were searched, and lots of shouting and beatings took place. It was late at night before our guards regained command of the camp, our cooks were allowed to get us some food and we got back to normal. Thorough as the search was, the radio they were seeking was in a service water bottle which had a tube down the centre filled with water, and although they handled it and threw it to the floor, they didn't find it. It was a good job that the stupid 'Ingeris' won that round.

The lads who had been working in the string factory had been 'doing naughties'. In order to produce their daily quota of grams, they had wound on a few feet of rope gauge in the middle of the spool while the Nips were not around. Now came the test, as unbeknown to them, this string had now got to be made into rice packs. With thicknesses varying from cotton to rope, this presented a few problems. The outcome was that because so much thick stuff was smuggled out of the factory for disposal, the number of packs didn't tally with the weight of string used – a mystery far beyond the ability of the clever Nip soldier to work out.

Sacks made, we were now returned to Cycle Camp and Lieutenant Soni. As I had made myself useful at Glodok, I went to work for an Australian dentist; where Frank Graham had his own practice in England, this bloke was a regular Army man. All I can say is I would rather have toothache than let him do anything about it!

This stay at Soni Boy's camp was only of a few weeks' duration, as a new draft was assembled and when we were paraded for the glass-rod test, we knew that we were bound for a sea journey. Before such trips, Japanese medical staff took stool samples by means of inserting a glass rod into one's back passage. Dysentery was a dreaded disease on these occasions, and they also didn't trust 'Ingeris' not to tender samples from known sufferers in order to avoid going on the drafts.

Preliminaries over, we were moved out on 6 June 1944 to the ship. We had heard from lads who had survived these transports of the hellish conditions, so we were not surprised with what we encountered.

As we assembled to leave Cycle Camp, a rumour was passed to us at the last minute that the Allies had landed in France. Again, we hoped that it was true. Alas, under the circumstances we were even more inclined to the belief that it was just a cruel morale-booster.

We clambered down into the hold of the ship, being hurried by guards waving sticks. There was a shelf all around the hold, 3ft off the ground, and we were allocated sufficient space to sit on our haunches and were five-deep on and under the shelf. Once all in, a grid was closed over the hold, which meant that if we were bombed or torpedoed we stood no chance.

The food was scarce, and it would be polite to call it awful. We were allowed up for the toilet in turn, twice a day. The facilities comprised a huge wooden box roped over the side of the ship, with a board removed from the bottom to allow you to stand astride it. Upon returning to one's space, someone would ask: 'Did you flush the loo?'

By the time the boat was ready to sail, we were due to be introduced to the delights of the chef. As I had been fortunate enough, or crafty enough, to secure a space on the front row, I was beckoned to go up and collect the usual rice and what was called tea. We were passing the boom at the exit from the harbour now, and had the unusual sight of two German U-boats which were leaving at the same time.

Life in the hold was getting more and more uncomfortable, what with the heat and the noise and vibration from the engines. We sailed on through the night in total darkness, and as fumes began to affect some of the lads and visits to toilets became essential, many unpleasant incidents with the guards occurred.

During the next day, there appeared to be fewer restrictions on visits to the deck, providing people didn't hang about unduly and numbers were kept down. Realizing the situation, we decided to go up in an organized rota, taking turns around the hold.

Just after dark on the first day, we were all made to stay below, and as we heard the engines racing and slowing we could only guess at what was happening. The obvious theory was that we were evading an attack, and as it was dark, it must be submarines. All of a sudden there was an unholy bump, which echoed all around the hold. Everyone was startled and reacted in various ways, from panic to prayers.

Up top, all we could hear was shouting Nips, and as they were in no panic we assumed all was in order. What had happened was that we had tied up on a dock-side – something we had not bargained for so soon. I have no idea how long that episode lasted, but I do know that it was not one of the more enjoyable experiences of my life.

When we set off at dawn the following day, we had all resigned ourselves to the routine of life on a prison ship, but unfortunately some of the lads were becoming affected by fumes and were quite sick. When any water was required for cleaning, it had to be hauled up in a bucket from the sea. We had no doctor available, and the task of looking after the sick and keeping the place as clean as possible not only kept us occupied, but was also vitally important if we were to stand any chance of surviving a long journey under these conditions.

The worst of our immediate fears were relieved when we found ourselves ordered to disembark at Singapore. We found we were again tied up behind a U-boat, and as we were hustled off the ship into a huge warehouse, the German sailors used a wind-up gramophone to play an English wartime song, 'We're gonna hang out the washing on the Siegfried Line'. They appeared to be quite happy, waving to us with thumbs-up signs, and our guards went to great lengths to hustle us out of their view. Some of us began to wonder if the story of the Allies landing in Europe was true, but the more pessimistic decided that the Jerries were just taking the Mickey. (History now knows that the optimists were right.)

We eventually marched to a huge PoW camp of *attap* huts (made from palm fronds), with sleeping shelves about 3ft off the floor. As we were settling in, the lads already in the camp were providing a meal for us. Although it was the customary rice, soup and tea, to have it cooked with care by our own kin was like coming home to mother's cooking.

Hardly had I started on my meal when I heard a recognizable voice, and limping into view came Andy Berry shouting, 'Where's Jimmy Banton?' He had almost kept his promise of heading for home at the first sign of trouble. On his way to a Ceylon-bound ship, he had stopped for an extra drink, and as he ran to get back on the lorry, he slipped, broke his ankle and went to hospital, and so became a PoW instead.

It transpired that it was only intended for us to spend a couple of days here before moving on, but alas the best-laid plans of mice and men – and even Japs – often go astray. On our first night in Singapore, we heard the sound of air-raid sirens once again. We were delighted to hear bombs dropping and guns firing – now we knew someone was trying to get us home. The Japs, obviously not as happy as we were, were in utter panic. We were not in any immediate danger; apart, that is, from trigger-happy guards who could go berserk with the slightest provocation.

We had to stay and work tidying up the docks, and all marvelled at the accuracy of the bombing of the shipping. In later years, I have come to wonder if it was an air raid or a daring mission by sea by Aussie commandos. I will never know, but I do know that the Japs were very touchy from that night on.

The time came to continue our journey. There was no marching to the docks this time, as we were put on lorries with an armed guard on each one. To our surprise, we boarded open pleasure boats – obviously only a short trip, but where to?

We eventually entered the mouth of a river which wound its way into dense jungle. This, we learned, was Sumatra. The noise of the boat disturbed the wildlife: monkeys screeched, birds fled, and there was a new experience, with crocodiles scuttling up the banks from the river as we approached.

A small landing stage appeared and we tied up alongside it. Seeing a huge pile of railway lines and sleepers, nobody needed two guesses as to what our new purpose in life was to be, but we did not know just what was ahead for us.

We walked about half-a-mile along a railway track to a small collection of *attap* huts and settled ourselves in. It transpired that a workforce of natives had gone ahead of us, hacking a clearing through what until now had been virgin jungle. Our first few days were spent doing odd jobs, particularly loading bogies with rails and sleepers, ready to start the work of building what we were told was to be 250 miles of railway.[4]

As the days passed, more men continued to arrive and eventually it was time to start our task. When we got into full swing it worked out as follows. One team of rail-layers would build a stretch of about 25 miles and move to a new camp. Another team stayed at base camp, unloading rails from ferries and reloading to supply the layers. Later, the camp of layers would split up; half would go ahead again, laying a further stretch, whilst the rest added finishing touches to what had already been laid, building slip-roads for passing of trains etc.

There were no mechanical aids apart from the diesel lorries used as locos. These were six-wheeled, German-built vehicles which could have their road-wheels exchanged for rail-wheels. With everything having to be manhandled, this very quickly became a daunting task. As we had by now had more than two years of hard work and starvation rations, men

---

[4] The Sumatra Railway.

soon became victims of exhaustion and disease. We were after all building along the equator.

The gang at base camp would load rails onto two bogies (see diagram at end of chapter). Sufficient sleepers, spikes and fish-plates, bolts etc. for the length of rails would be placed on top – all having to be manhandled.

The laying gang was divided into two sub-gangs, each with their own job. The first team took off the spikes, which were in baskets, and laid them along in readiness. The second team carried the sleepers, one man to each, and laid them in position, then came the rail-carriers, using whatever they could find to pad their shoulders. To shouts of 'two-six-up' (and rude variations), they would lift, carry and drop rails into place, working from either side of the bogie. Each rail would be spiked only at the ends, and the bogies propelled forward after about three lengths were down. As each bogie was unloaded, it would be derailed and pushed out of the way. When the train had passed, a gang would line up the unspiked sleepers, fasten them down and tighten the fish-plate bolts, which up to now were only finger-tight. All off-loaded bogies would then have to be re-railed and the engine would return them to be refilled. If all odd jobs were completed to the Nips' satisfaction before the next train (which was waiting in a siding) arrived, we had a *Yasumi* (Japanese for rest). The chance of this of course improved the further we were from the base or siding. Because we had a set distance to lay each day, this was a 'catch 22' situation. The longer we rested, the later we got back to camp. Everything was against our survival now, not only poor diet, but the jungle with its diseases and our physical exhaustion. We were without clothing or footwear, and people were getting sores from untreated cuts and blisters, trapped feet and hands.

The Japs demanded their number of workers each day, and would fetch out the sick if we were short. Under these conditions, we found that we left behind a higher number of graves at each camp. These cemeteries we marked with large wooden crosses, in the hope that they could be found some day later before the jungle reclaimed the land.

The further we advanced, the worse the situation became. To add to our problems, the guards became more hostile; we assumed that the war was not going as well for them as they thought it should.

We also suspected that the native workforce had evaporated in some way or other. As we moved to each camp along the line, we were occupying the huts which they had built and left behind, and now we were finding corpses in them which had to be removed and disposed of before we could use them. Just one more health hazard.

Adding further weight to this theory was the fact that we now had to build our own bridges. The only good fortune in this was that a fair amount of timber had been felled and prepared before the natives vanished. Bridge building was a real hazard. The piles were driven by hauling up a huge weight by pulley block and tripod and letting it drop onto the pile. All hell and a lot of hard work was the penalty if you missed and the weight went into the river.

A couple of my worst experiences involved bridges. A huge party of us were taken to a bridge over a very wide river, where flooding had dislodged some piles and caused the bridge to bend. The main damage, fortunately, was to the piles at the water's edge, which had been swept away and the rails and sleepers were hanging in mid-air. We were given the task of building up piles of sleepers criss-cross fashion to support them.

Amidst a lot of Japanese hostility, work began to get under way. It was late in the day when we had any food, and it was made clear that we would stay until the work was completed. When darkness fell, we were given scores of torches made of rubber wrapped in dried leaves.

The real ordeal came when we were up in the air, well and truly hungry and exhausted, and the monsoon started. The wind and rain extinguished the torches and we could not find our way down, so we had to cling there – unclothed, freezing and petrified – for several hours until the storm subsided and daylight came.

True to their words, we were not allowed back to camp by the guards, but had a couple of hours' sleep in the open air. After a meal of rice, we started again. We worked all day and through the next night. During the second night, it was only the cold and river torrents (plus the Japs and mosquitoes) which we had to endure. At one point, three Nip engineers were on a pontoon jabbering away when one of the lads untied the mooring rope. Amazingly, although they were despatched to the raging torrents, their loss did not appear to be even noticed. We never heard a word about it.

It was a couple more days before the work was complete and we returned to camp. True to their unpredictable character, the Japs gave us a day off work and extra rice rations. It was standard practice that any extra food went into the kitty, a scheme we practised because the Japs only allowed half-rations for the sick and we insisted on equal shares.

On another occasion when bridge-building, we had a real pantomime. We had just returned from a day of rail-laying and were being counted upon arrival at the camp guard-room. Out came a Jap sergeant we had nicknamed 'Dracula', who was the most hated swine of the lot, carrying his usual pick-axe shaft. He chopped off the end two columns of five, and then he took me forward and said, 'You, *Ancho*' (foreman). That meant I was first in line for any trouble. As we were taken away, the lads shouted consoling remarks to the effect that they would tell our folks what happened to us when they got home.

We loaded up one of the engine–cum-lorries with axes, saws, jacks etc., and some rice, tea and soup, and with the Jap sergeant driving, off we went. Our scene of operation was a collapsed bridge, this time only a small one, and one of its cross members had given notice. The replacement timber was at this stage still growing.

To our surprise, 'Dracula' told us to eat first and gave each of us a cigarette. The tree was felled, and the beam cut to size without any problems. Next we jacked up the rails and changed the timbers, and Dracula worked as well. He gave us several rest periods, and for the first night since we met him was a human being.

It was early morning when we loaded up and tried to set off home, but alas, the wagon would not start. Several attempts at push-starting all failed, and we set off to walk back.

Along the way we came to a Jap site, and a steam loco in the siding was almost in full steam. After a lot of jabbering, we climbed onto it. As the *Ancho*, I was on the footplate with Dracula while the others hung on the side. My 'first-class' ride meant that I had to add a few logs of wood into the engine.

When we got back to camp, the next day's work party was lining up; we had a mug of rice and a cup of tea and had to join them. Dracula was on parade, ready to go with them, when he saw me. Through the interpreter, we said we would rather go than eleven sick men have to go in our place. Dracula quite liked this, and said he would go eleven short (for the first time ever) and we must go back to camp. He often made me his *Ancho* afterwards, and no one ever understood why we never seemed to have trouble; 'Wwho could understand their tiny warped minds anyway?

Each day that went by saw us getting weaker and weaker. Each day someone died, and some of the sick were on occasions sent back to the base camp. Here, an excuse for a hospital was supposed to exist, but an equivalent number of people also had to be found to replace those brought in. The food in all camps consisted of boiled rice and tea for breakfast, then steamed rice and a stew made from unripe bananas and their flowers at midday and in the evening. The stew thus produced was a blue mess the consistency of paint, and was christened 'Blue Danube'. When it travelled out to working parties on the engines, it acquired the flavour of the diesel oil. When time permitted, we would gather leaves and grass to make a boil-up of our own; not only did this taste better than 'Blue Danube', it was also said to contain more vitamins.

Of course, as the railway progressed, maintaining it became a problem. Because the sleepers were made from green timber, the ants ate the underside of them and we would have to replace them. Jacking up the rails and renewing and repacking sleepers was perhaps harder work than laying track. It also brought with it another boring and laborious task, that of providing sand to be used as ballast.

Digging sand was the job I hated most of all. The task was one cubic metre per man per day, dug from the bank into baskets, carried and loaded into trucks. Nips would stake out the area at the start of the day, but they invariably got short-change because we would move the pegs if we got half a chance. If he caught us he would move it the other way, but we won about 10-1 on that one!

Christmas 1944 came and went with only one day off work to mark its passing – no extra rice this time.

Apart from regular bouts of malaria, I was lucky enough to suffer only one dose of dysentery, which fortunately I shook off. It may sound ridiculous, but the main treatment was to be starved. Some people could not abide the golden rule and made things worse for themselves; some even paid the ultimate price of their lives. I was a coward and wanted to come home, so I accepted the advice. Dysentery, malaria and malnutrition were the causes of most of our losses. The only thing we could do to keep ourselves going was to pay every attention possible to hygiene.

Each camp was alongside a river, which was to be the water supply. The area upstream was kept for collecting drinking and cooking water, with downstream for bathing and further down for 'dobbie' (laundry) of clothing. Clothing comprised a loincloth, usually made from rice sacking, and a pair of 'Scholl-like' sandals, homemade from scrounged materials. Soap, of course, was an item of long-past luxury. All in all, hygiene was a problem, but life depended on it. The huts were ridden with bugs, and these had to be endured and accepted as part of life in the tropics – the jungle was no exception to that.

The Japs at one place decided to build a rail-line down to the edge of the river in order to supply steam locos with water. This was done, and a 'Heath Robinson'-type water-crane built. The locos they were using were huge 2-6 types with large cow-catchers on them. The first loco came with much Japanese interest and excitement, and a party of PoWs ready to do the crane work. As all the 'stupid Ingeris' soldiers forecast, the sand-supported track gave way and the huge loco toppled over on its side. Japanese excitement was now of a different kind, and at these times we had learned that it was wise to tread very carefully.

Never daunted, we had to return the loco to its upright position. This task, which was started on the following day, was the achievement of the impossible. All available jacks were collected and placed in position. As each inch of lift was made, it was packed up, and this went on for days. Because visits were made by irate Jap engineers, the guards and the grease monkeys became very touchy, and we were at the bottom of the list where the luck stopped. We endured some very unpleasant scenes, and long days and nights of work. When the loco began to lift, some pulley blocks were brought into action to assist. Anticipating what would happen to these wires if anything went wrong, I made sure I worked out of their sphere if possible. Twice the obvious happened and we had casualties; fortunately the only fatality was one of our hosts, and although this heightened the tension, it was better than losing another of our own. The loco was eventually righted, but before the task was completed, one stupid Nip was on the footplate attempting to fire it up – something I was not altogether keen on. Although I one day hoped to go to heaven, I did not fancy arriving there on a cloud of steam accompanied by some stupid Nip!

On and on we went, on what seemed to be an endless task. Among the worst days and worst fits of guards, we kept our cool. Those who had lost heart (as I nearly did before meeting Jack Brown) had fallen by the wayside, and those of us left made sure we didn't suffer the same fate. We all became accustomed and immune to guards' tantrums; we accepted them as part of life and treated them with the contempt which their ignorance deserved.

We saw no one other than our fellows and our guards. We had no news and knew nothing of the outside world. Our rescuers could be a million miles away or about to enter our camps for all we knew. Furthermore, no news from home ever reached camps on the Sumatra railways; camps in dense jungle from which it was futile to attempt an escape – so remote that fires had to be lit at night to deter wildlife such as tigers. On one occasion, a small herd of elephants did pass through, but no one was hurt.

The routine became so monotonous, and we all had our ideas how it would end. No one doubted we would win the war. My belief was that it could, for all we know, end tomorrow.

Work parties began to think that the guards were becoming human, and that they were as fed up as us with a life in limbo that was not much fun for them either.

The work party were all lined up to start work one day, but after standing around for some time we were returned to camp without explanation for *Yasumi*. Apart from Christmas Day, this was the first day this had happened since we arrived in Sumatra. This procedure was repeated for a few days, but I was taking my turn on 'in camp' work – it was my luck to have to work. Then we were told not to prepare more work parties until they were requested, and so everyone joked that the war must have ended.

Some days later, a native appeared in the camp as if he had fallen from the blue sky, as no others had been seen for months. He shouted at the top of his voice, '*Senso Abiss*' (Indonesian for 'War finished'), then he disappeared as quickly as he came. (I later had a theory about him.) After giving this some thought, and in view of recent happenings, the senior British officer, whose name I can't recall, approached the Jap Commandant, saying: 'I believe the war has ended and if so, I demand food and medicine for my men.' At this the Jap drew his sword and struck out at him, and he made a 'tactical withdrawal'. To his surprise, and relief, he was not pursued. Later that morning, a letter written in Japanese was taken to him by the Jap guard sergeant. News of this went through the camp like wildfire, and all kind of speculation was rife.

An hour or so later, we were called together; English-speaking in one hut, Dutch-speaking in another. The translation was read to us: the war was over. It was also requested that the Japanese be protected by thirty PoWs – for this there were many volunteers, but our officers turned down the request. It was ordered that there should be no singing and celebrating.

To overcome the 'no singing' order, for fear of causing trigger-happy guards to panic, we stood and said the words of the Lord's Prayer and the national anthem, then had a silent prayer of our own before our CO spoke. He congratulated everyone for the spirit which had been fostered during our ordeal, then asked us to uphold our dignity and to prove to Japanese and Dutch alike that British troops were supreme. Promising to keep us informed immediately of all news as soon as it arrived, he wished us good luck in the rest of our lives and dismissed us. Unrehearsed, and although he was without headgear, as one man we all saluted him, and as he said 'Thank you' and returned the salute, I am sure he was in tears. How I wish I could remember his name.

The rest of the day is beyond my description. The 'no singing' order was a waste of time, because no one could even speak. Everyone walked around or just sat around. We shook each hand and patted each shoulder, but words would not come. Tears were everywhere – most were tears of joy, although as we had no news from home for more than three-and-a-half years, many were in fear of what we were soon to learn.

It must be remembered that when we last had received any news, Britain was still being heavily bombed. Were our towns and homes still standing? Were our loved ones still alive? Were our brothers and pals who were fighting still alive?

The first tragedy brought about by our new-found freedom was the loss of nineteen of our lads, who either gave up their fight against illness or simply could not stand the shock. This was the biggest single-day loss of our railway ordeal.

Some food was produced, but few were even interested in it. So the day progressed, and when darkness fell most of us retreated to our huts, which were illuminated (if that is not an overstatement) by a couple of bits of string stuck in a shell full of palm oil. A Welshman named Williams said: 'If they want to shoot anybody for singing it can be me.' He started, and soon everyone joined in.

Eventually we all moved outside, stoked up the fires and had a good sing-song. The cook-house produced tea and made rice balls, and we sat there all night. No guards ventured in, and I can't recall seeing them again, although we stayed quite a few days longer. Our officers opened the Nip food stores and our diet was made a little more palatable with the addition of soya beans, sugar, salt and even a little dried fish.

At last a train of trucks came to the camp. We were the most advanced camp on the line, and native chaps were crewing it. We had not managed to join a gang coming to meet us from the north, as we were supposed to do.

After carefully loading our sick onto the last trucks (in order to keep them from the sparks of the wood-burning engine), we crammed tighter than sardines onto the remainder. The discomfort was not even noticed, and as the train moved off, a huge cheer went up and we were on our way home.

Note: Modern maps of Sumatra show two pieces of railway not joined together.

Picture:

Two bogies joined together with rails, with sleepers on top then baskets of bolts and fish-plates.

Chapter 5

Homeward Bound

A lthough every one of us was excited to be on the way home, there was a quiet air of apprehension. First of all, because we were at the most advanced camp along the rail line, we were last to be withdrawn to the base camp.

There was not even a cheer as we moved off, leaving empty huts, such utensils as were there, but saddest of all a large wooden cross standing guard over the graves of quite a few of our colleagues.

I was not alone in my doubts as to how some of the wooden bridges we would have to cross would stand up to the weight of the heavy loco plus quite a heavy train (for that kind of structure). However, we were much relieved, at the first deserted camp we reached, to find two of the small diesel locos waiting. The train was halved and we felt much happier now. It transpired that our officers at base camp had insisted on this as a safety precaution.

As we passed each deserted camp, they all looked the same. Even in the tropical sunshine, to me they appeared cold and damp, and at each one stood the tell-tale wooden cross. Some of these were adorned with wreaths, roughly made from the local vegetation – a last farewell gesture from their comrades.

After we arrived at our destination, base camp, one who could not come to terms with her new found freedom was Judy, the camp's pet dog. Judy had been taught to lie quiet and concealed in a sack during previous moves, because once seen by the guards she would have been destroyed. Judy had been injured in action, twice shipwrecked and survived along with us. She was eventually to be awarded the 'Animal VC' and became the subject of a novel entitled *Judy*.

Everyone was looking for friends and there were many happy reunions, but of course also the sad news of others.

Food was already prepared for us, although still the same diet. Whilst I was eating, my old pal Jack Brown came to find me. Jack had been sunk on his way to Sumatra, and spent two days and nights on a raft prior to being picked up by a Jap ship, only because he was in the company of a Jap survivor. Jack, who had stayed at base camp working among the sick, said, 'Come across and have a chat when you get settled. I'll have to go because I'm up to the neck in it.'

I went to see Jack – and a sight to make one weep. There were men like skeletons, sick and dying, lying on the ground in the most appalling conditions. As yet no aid had arrived, and the medics were performing miracles. They were all working, and had been for months, night and day taking turns to snatch a few minutes' sleep. How they kept it up will always remain a mystery to me.

'Do you want a job, Jim?' Jack asked. The question did not even warrant an answer, and I stayed and helped until we were relieved. The worst part was to see people die for the want of a little medicine, and yet the war was over.

Being on Dutch territory, they assumed the role of organizing the evacuation and amassed piles of bumf; and the system, true to form, greatly favoured the home side.

It appeared that a couple of intelligence officers accompanied by two native carriers had visited the camp. They had been put ashore from a submarine and been watching the situation. I later wondered if the chap who ran into our camp was one such person, because we saw no other natives in all our months there.

Next we had a visit from Lord and Lady Mountbatten (Mountbatten was Supreme Allied Commander of South-East Asia Command), and a small but valuable supply of medicine arrived. Being in such a remote place, it was difficult to get to us at all, so life did not improve.

Out of the blue arrived three lorries; how they got there remains a mystery to me. In charge was an RAF nursing officer standing about 5ft nothing and as smart as a new pin. All the elaborate Dutch plans were thrown to one side. 'Five stretcher cases and ten walking on each lorry,' she said. When the Dutch CO started to intervene, she waved him away. 'Start here,' she said, pointing to the end of the hut, 'and work through in order; don't waste time and let's have these lads where they can get treatment.' Us English were delighted with this angel – particularly us RAF people.

The lorries went to a field, where the patients were loaded onto Dakotas and flown to Singapore. With the shuttle service set up, food and medicine arrived, and within two or three days the sick were all evacuated. There was space on the last lorries, and Jack was told to jump on. 'Not without my mate,' he said, and as I had helped I was put aboard as well. We didn't even have time to say farewell to our pals; they, incidentally, came out by boat some days later.

On the flight to Singapore, an old Dutchman looked into the cockpit and found it all deserted, with just the control column moving slowly back and fore. He hadn't heard of 'George', the automatic pilot, and he just passed out, causing a few moments diversion.

When we arrived at Singapore, we knew for certain that we were free. There were planes of all kinds – Spitfires with five-bladed propellers and things we had never seen or heard of before. We were overwhelmed by the attention paid to us. We could have as many cups of tea as we liked, but only two rounds of bread and butter to eat – to us that was a feast, as it was almost four years since we had seen bread. This was supplied from a mobile canteen run by FANY (the First Aid Nursing Yeomanry), who were similar to the Red Cross.

Next came a trip across Singapore, and a look at a few places which we recalled, to what was now known as 35 British General Hospital. When the Japs took Singapore, they massacred most of the patients and staff in this place. That was all in the past now, and we were given a bath or shower, pyjamas, and allocated to a clean bed with white sheets and even pillows. We were all weighed and then given a light meal. I weighed in at 6 stone 4lb.

The Red Cross came to visit us with gifts of combs and other materials, but primarily pencil and paper to write home. We were requested to write immediately, and letters would leave for England that night. This was exactly one month after VJ Day.

We spent the second day enjoying the luxury of radio and newspapers, and had visits from all sorts of people who tried to pamper us all they could. Late at night, a group of us were still up and about, some playing cards, when in came an Army MO and his team. He selected twenty of us to fly out as far as Colombo, Ceylon (now Sri Lanka), on a couple of Sunderlands which were going unladen.

We were sent to a storeroom and kitted out in jungle-green uniform and a pair of heavy army 'ammo' boots. After a light meal, we were taken down to the seaplane base and were drinking mugs of tea. The door opened and in walked a small group of officers wearing more red braid and medal ribbons than would sink a ship. As we chatted quite merrily to these chaps, Jack Brown questioned the most decorated one about how he came to acquire all his fancy work – only to learn a few minutes later from one of his aides that he was no less than a general (I can't remember, but I think it was Auchinleck, the commander-in-chief in India, although I could be wrong).

It was now dawn, and we boarded some small boats and were taken out to the Sunderlands. On board, the crew made us welcome and we were soon taxiing out for take-off. Landing and taking off in flying boats is a wonderful experience. Once airborne, we were told to help ourselves to whatever food we wanted, and a couple of the lads soon got busy in the galley.

After a meal, I decided to take a lilo bed to the stern of the vessel and get some sleep. I was awakened and offered a cuppa as we were soon due to land in Ceylon. In a building on the quayside, an English meal of beef and the trimmings was ready for us, but I had become airsick due to the swinging of the stern end of the vessel, thus I had to refuse the first full meal on offer, much to the amusement of the rest of the lads. A couple of tablets later I was as well as the others when we were taken by luxury coach to board a Red Cross train on our way to Colombo.

The journey on this train was beyond belief. Here we were, three days ago in the jungle and living on rice amidst all the ill and dying lads, now sleeping in white sheets, clean pyjamas, clean shaven; and more than that, a nice nurse to tuck us up. If you as much as turned over during the night, you would find a nurse at your side. Everyone was so good to us that it was embarrassing. We had breakfast on the train, and late that morning arrived at Colombo. Fruit and drinks were on offer before we boarded a couple of buses which took us along the coast to a military hospital – we were already half-way home.

This hospital stood in spacious, well-tended grounds and was on a beautiful tropical beach – palm trees, rolling surf, the lot. The first thing was a meal, and then we were to send a free cable home. People here could not do enough for us. We were told that we could have whatever we asked for – and we got it too.

During the afternoon, a couple of PR officers came and gave us some insight of what to expect when we got back to England, and most of it sounded queer to us. Then all manner of people came in and out to chat – civilians, service people, etc. – and all brought gifts of fruit, chocolate, cigarettes and such like, although there was an abundance of said things already here.

This went on until late evening, and then a couple of Medical Officers came to give us a once over and lots of good advice on how to take care of ourselves on the way back to fitness. They said we could go to the kitchen and get a meal at any hour of the day or night, and advised us to eat there as it would be food which would not harm us.

The following day, a group of WAAFs and Wrens came to us and offered to take us into Colombo. This they did each day whilst we were there, as they were cypher clerks whose work was not needed now.

On the first day, Jack, myself and one other lad went to the cinema with three WAAFs and saw a film, *For Whom the Bell Tolls*. Everyone knew by our colour who we were, and no one would take money, so it again became embarrassing to go into shops. Cinemas were different, I didn't mind that. We returned for tea time and spent the evening writing letters, etc.

We sometimes spent our days in Colombo with these hostesses or on the beach, however the mood took us.

A couple of days after we had sent our telegrams, the officer who had been ordered to look after us asked if anyone had not heard from home. I hadn't. 'See to that, Sergeant Major,' he said to one of his aides, and later that day I had a reply from Dorothy, soon to be followed by the first one which had gone astray.

We were 'condemned' to this life of luxury for about six weeks, because what transport did call at Colombo was already filled by people who had been boarded further out. Our flying start had got our small party nowhere fast. I myself was not sorry about this really, because it gave me time to gain some weight and grow some hair. Apart from being yellow-skinned due to mepacrine tablets, I looked something like a human being when I arrived home.

As we sat talking in our room one morning, a female voice in the corridor was calling 'Where's Jim Banton?' I'm sure I broke into a frozen sweat, wondering if it was one of my sisters or even Dorothy who had joined the services – I didn't at that split second recall I had already heard from Dorothy at home. Alas, in came a major of the QAIMNSR (Queen Alexandra's Imperial Military Nursing Service Reserve), who was Sister Perry whom we at No. 11 knew from the Isolation Hospital at Burton. As she was due to fly home the following day, she promised to let my folks at home know I was OK – I can't recall that she did.

On another occasion I went down with malaria. Although we had come to learn to live with this (and even work after the first day), to these medics I was seriously ill. Regular temperature checks and heaven knows what fuss was made. When the day staff handed over to the night staff, a little dark-haired nurse said, 'I'll come and give you a cool bed-bath and clean bed when we have done our rounds.' I thought, 'Like hell you will'. Jack got me some clean pyjamas and changed my bed whilst I nipped off for a quick shower. In comes the nurse, and when she sees what has happened – talk about panic, she even called the doctor in and he told me how ill I was. At this, all the lads started at him and he told us that we were all 'bloody crazy!' The next day, I was in the cafe on the beach with the lads, when the doctor came in – he got used to us in time.

Coming from Colombo one night, Jack and I went to beg a lift off some sailors. They were all drunk as a monkey, and the one in charge said if we drove them back to camp, they would fix us up. Jack volunteered me for the job, and when we delivered them, they loaned us a car to get home, which was in the early hours of the morning.

In the grounds of the hospital were the graves of two unknown Japanese airmen, shot down during a raid. Some of the lads made a practice of watering these as they came in late at night!

Then came the day we were to start our last leg of the journey home. Having been given some kit at the local RAF camp, we had some packing to do for the first time; another new experience. There is a photo of our small party with the two sisters who had looked after us, taken as we left.

We went to Colombo to board the *Highland Monarch*, a refrigerator ship captured from the Germans. There was pandemonium here because some civilians from Hong Kong had been given a lift to England on the understanding that the cabins were reserved for us. There were women and a couple of children among them, and they were not keen on giving way to troops (a typical attitude of these people pre-war). One of our lads said to one of the officers, 'If this ship is going to England, just get it going, we will sleep anywhere.' A chorus of agreement settled that, and we got down below. We were on our way!

The journey through the Indian Ocean and Red Sea was a mundane sea voyage. The ship, although acceptably comfortable, had no luxuries such as swimming pool and concert hall, like we enjoyed on the *Stirling Castle* on our way out. On the other hand, we did not have to care about submarines or aircraft. We passed away the days basking in the sunshine, reading and listening to the ship's radio and so on.

We had the cruiser *Belfast* come alongside on a couple of days, and it entertained us with its band for an hour or so. The *Belfast* is now moored on the Thames as a museum.

One daily job which I set myself was to visit the ship's shops and purchase items which we had been told were in short supply at home, such as jam, tinned fruit, cigarettes, etc. I had acquired a couple of huge navy kitbags, and proceeded to stack them to the top in tiers, innocently and stupidly making for myself a problem of weight.

During the past three-and-a-half years, I, and I suppose everyone else, had dreamed and visualized what would happen when we arrived amongst our relatives and friends. Such thoughts blocked out the monotony of the repetitive and soul-destroying jobs for many hours. Now, as I got close to that moment, I spent the vacant times doing what I can only describe as a mental dress rehearsal for it.

Things became more interesting as we entered the Suez Canal. We could see people and villages alongside, and wrecks of ships which had been lifted out of the canal lay rusting on its banks. The canal is a wonderful piece of engineering, accomplished in the days before bulldozers, etc.

We made our one and only call, at Suez, and we went ashore only to collect some uniform blue in readiness for arriving home in November. Then it was on through the Mediterranean, and as the temperature dropped we gradually resorted to our blue and khaki. Now we were Army and Air Force again, and it was strange, somehow we all felt proud of our own force and these uniforms. The odd-ball gang of naked PoWs had evolved into a green and khaki gang of nomads, and into fully fledged and proud members of His Majesty's Forces.

As we passed through the Straits of Gibraltar, with the imposing sight of the Rock towering up and dwarfing our little *Highland Monarch*, everyone was now in winter gear, and the navy-blue of the crew had joined the colour scheme. The ship's captain came on the tannoy, as he had often done before, but this time he said, 'Once passed this rock, we turn right and we are three days from Southampton.'

Up the English Channel, the sea was calm and the sun shone. We were now preparing our kit for disembarking, and I was relieved to learn that arrangements had been made for all our luggage and we would only have to handle our hand luggage.

Early on the third day, we had our first sight of the coast of England. It was 9 November, and we docked at Southampton soon after midday.

During the process of docking, we had a couple of disappointments surrounding a moment for which we had all waited for so long. We had heard of early PoWs being greeted with bands playing on the dockside and relatives waiting for them. For us, there was just an untidy dockside, and the few people who were around had a typical Friday afternoon attitude towards their tasks. I think this was more something different to what we had been told to expect than a disappointment; after all, the war as far as these people were concerned had been over six months ago. They had seen it all before, as thousands of troops had come home, some for a month's leave and some for demob. As for PoWs, we were among the late arrivals and, as troops go, only a small contingent.

When the gangplank was in position, up came the Disembarkation Officer and his retinue. About half an hour elapsed, and then the tannoy came into action and he announced that no one would disembark until the following day – that was a disappointment, and was greeted with much abuse; very much abuse.

While everyone had been asking for reasons and creating a furore, a further party had come aboard unnoticed. Again the tannoy crackled open and everyone quietened. This time the attitude was totally different. An Air Commodore introduced himself and said he had come on behalf of HM the King to welcome us home, to which he added his own greetings. He then extended greetings to the forty-five RAF personnel from all members of the RAF, and told us to prepare to disembark in 15 minutes' time. We would travel by train to London for an overnight stop, and proceed the following day to RAF Cosford for dispersal.

As we hurriedly said our farewells to our Army pals, we made our way to two awaiting coaches, whilst a party of Army lads loaded our kit onto a lorry. An RAF Flight Lieutenant was our guide to London, and while we waited on Southampton station for our train, the Rail Transport Officer came out and said we had to return to the docks as we had not been through Customs. No one was in favour of this, and several rude messages were offered as a reply.

On arrival at quite a nice hotel in the city, a good tea was served and later an evening dinner. A handful of lads decided to have a look around London during the evening, but the majority were quite happy to have a quiet drink and an early night.

The following morning, Saturday, after an early breakfast, the two coaches arrived to take us to the station. Whilst we were boarding the coaches, the driver of the lorry which was carrying our kit was asking, 'Where is LAC Banton?' I thought one of my kit bags had burst under the strain, but to my relief he only wanted to know why they were so heavy. The bright answer was proffered by one of the gang: 'Because they are full.'

On we went to Wolverhampton, where a work party was on hand to transfer our kit to the train for Cosford. Although Cosford station is only a couple of hundred yards from the camp main gate, buses collected us. Our first job was to deposit our hand luggage in a wooden dormitory and go into the dining hall. Officers and men wandered amongst us as we ate, and made us feel back in our own 'mob'.

At Singapore, we had been amazed by the new RAF, but that was nothing compared to what we were now seeing. We were divided into three groups of fifteen, and went on differing routes through medical, records, accounts, interrogation and awards (for medal ribbons). For the payment of 9*d* (old money) each, we were supplied with labels for the forwarding home of any luggage which we could not carry – the best 1/6*d* I ever spent. Another hot meal was supplied at tea time, and it was now after 5pm and dark.

As we were told that we would not be leaving camp that night, we returned to the billet to decide how to spend the evening. I had taken my shoes and shirt off, ready to go for a shower, when someone shouted: 'Two for Burton, one for Tamworth, can go tonight if you make it fast!'

We scrambled into a pick-up, me with my collar and tie in my pocket, and off to the station, followed by a motorcycle DR.[1] The train had gone, and the pick-up sped like a rally car to Wolverhampton while the DR returned to camp with the message.

At Wolverhampton station, half a dozen Army MPs were waiting for us and they took us through the crowded platforms to a train bound for Birmingham, which had been held up especially for us by the RTO.[2]

It was at Birmingham where our luck ran out. We could hear the Burton train announced, but as the crowd was so dense, we could not get to it in time and we had to wait an hour and a half for the next one.

Finally on the Burton train, we shared a compartment with some Army lads. By the time Burton was reached, only two soldiers and two FEPOWS (Far East PoWs) were left.

Coming out of the station at Burton, the streets were deserted and dimly lit. The deadly silence was almost eerie. One of the soldiers carried my kit bag for me, and as we passed Byrkley Street, the other lad and a couple of soldiers left us.

The homecoming plans which I had rehearsed mentally hundreds of times were already falling apart. At this stage, I was supposed to be in a

---

[1] Dispatch Rider – usually on a motorcycle.

[2] Rail Transport Officer – a service officer was sited at all large stations to assist troops with information and to confirm any delays which kept them from reaching units on time.

taxi with Dorothy and David heading for 78A. Instead, I was thanking a complete stranger for his help on the doorstep of No. 11.

It was now about 10pm, but doors weren't locked until retiring to bed in those days so I let myself in, complete with kit bag. As I undid my haversack from my back, my Dad heard and came in to see who it was. Poor old Dad, he didn't know which to do first – greet me or call my Mother; the result was he turned around about three times before he grabbed me around my neck and shouted, 'Mother!' Then, as his words wouldn't come, we made our way through to my Mother. As she got up to greet me, I was alarmed to discover that she had become crippled with arthritis.

Whilst we three chatted excitedly, Mother had made me a cup of coffee. Until now I had kept the promise which I had made to myself, not to lose my composure, but as I took the cup from my mother, I trembled like a leaf and had to put it down for a while. About five minutes had passed, and in came my sisters Margaret and Kathleen from a dance.

We had a little chat, and I got my act together before I set off for 78A, Dorothy and David, accompanied by my Father, who insisted on carrying my kit bag, just as a few years previously he had carried his own.

Along Victoria Crescent we went, and up the long dark path to No. 78A. I knocked on the door, and soon the head of Dorothy's Mother peered round, her long grey hair down around her shoulders as she was preparing for bed. Neither before or since have I seen a mouth open so wide with surprise – no one knew I was anywhere near home.

In went my Father and I, and met Dorothy's Father while her Mother vanished upstairs. In what seemed only seconds, down came Dorothy in dressing gown, hair in curlers and holding a newly awakened David. Here again, my vision of a passionate and private reunion was substituted by one witnessed by three of our four parents, which rather cramps one's style. The situation was retrieved, however, when Dorothy said to David, 'Who's this then?', and he said, 'It's my Daddy off the picture.'

My Dad left for home, and amongst tons of excitement and questions, I made my acquaintance with David, with the aid of a small amount of chocolate from a haversack which held more chocolate than he had seen in his entire life so far.

We chatted on excitedly until the early hours, all talking at the same time. David had long-since been returned to his slumbers. Dorothy and I were next to climb the wooden hill, closely followed by her Mother and Father.

I think it was sheer excitement (it was certainly nothing else!) which kept Dorothy and I awake. We lay whispering to each other as if we had to catch up on five years of life, and morning and breakfast came without either of us having a wink of sleep.

It was now Sunday, 11 November – Armistice Day. In a few hours, from noon on Friday to midnight on Saturday, what on earth had happened to me? Was it all true, or was I just dreaming? If so, I hoped not to wake up.

The RAF must take full marks for the efficiency which made this possible.

What about Dorothy and David, and the way her parents had cared for them in my stead, the long months of anxious waiting for them and both our families? What had been happening to them and the world while I had been completely cut off from all such knowledge?

From that morning onwards, those mysteries would unfold, but the one thing that was certain was that Dorothy and I were together now, joined by our first child and never to be parted again.

Chapter Six

Back Home

My first day at home was Armistice Sunday, which was a bright sunny, chilly, typical November day. Dorothy and I made plans for the priority of our visits, because as yet no one knew that I was home.

The things which I wanted to know about only came into conversations on occasions, and I had to learn little by little.

All of what I had daydreamed during the last almost four years was gradually proved to be far from reality. Dorothy's war had been just as difficult as had been my own.

I had thought of her during her pregnancy, being at home cared for and fussed over by her Mother and Father and everyone. The fact was that she had been very poorly right from the earliest days of her pregnancy. So ill did Dorothy become that her brother Lol was given twenty-eight days' leave from Ireland to be with her. This was, I imagine, a great help to Dorothy's Mother, because Lol sat up with her during the nights.

Dorothy's health deteriorated further, and in September she was admitted to Derbyshire Royal Infirmary with a severe kidney complaint, and was there, with the exception of a few days, until after David was born in February.

As if the critical illness was not sufficient to contend with, everything else was against her. Derby was a constant target for air raids, because Rolls-Royce engines – which were made there – were so vital to our war effort. During raids, the beds were pulled to the centre of the wards away from windows, and the rest was a game of chance. In semi-darkness, and with the noise of the anti-aircraft guns and bombs, this must have been a terrifying ordeal each time.

It must be remembered that at this time, telephones were a rare luxury, few and far between. Trains and buses were limited and always overcrowded, plus they were costly, and blackouts were also in operation. The consequence of these factors was that Dorothy had many days without visitors, and 99 per cent of visits were from her mother.

By the time Christmas came, Dorothy was no better. A new factor now came into the reckoning. The war in the Far East had started on 7 December, and already the situation was causing grave concern. I would not have blamed Dorothy one bit if she couldn't care less about that situation, but I know that she did and it certainly didn't help her. Thus my dreaming of Dorothy having her Christmas dinner at home in the love and company of her family was only that, a dream, and a million miles from the facts.

Nothing improved with the New Year, and the lack of news from or about me only had Dorothy worrying more, further hampering any progress in her own condition. It hurts me even now as often I think of what an ordeal this was for Dorothy. I am certain that at this stage she was suffering much more than me. For me it was just a matter of being chased through Malaya, Singapore, Sumatra and Java; at least I knew I was still alive and in one piece, and I was of the assumption that Dorothy was doing OK.

Dorothy was allowed home for a week in early February in the hope that the change would help her to prepare for the birth. Typical of Dorothy's parents, scarce as cash was, they fetched her home by taxi.

During the stay at home, a neighbour, Mr Godsby, sacrificed some of his meagre petrol ration to take her for a little ride around. Aunty Gladys would call round to help her take a bath, and on 14 February Dorothy returned to hospital at Derby.

On 24 February, Dorothy's mother went to pay her usual visit, and as she passed the office, the ward sister hailed her; she glanced into the ward and saw Dorothy propped up in bed. Dorothy watched as her mother was taken into the nursery to be introduced to her grandson, who had been born earlier that day.

From now on, Dorothy's health slowly improved and she was discharged from hospital in March, but had to travel back and forth to Derby for treatment. In April, I was reported 'missing', and some months later 'missing believed prisoner'. One day in April 1943, as Dorothy was readying herself for another trip to Derby, she had news that I was confirmed a PoW in Japanese hands. I suppose that under the circumstances, that could be considered good news. What certainly was good news was her discharge from hospital care.

As time went by, I learned more and more of how Dorothy existed during the war, and the overriding story was how much we both owe to the care and sacrifices of her Mother and Father. I learned of Lawrence sending money from North Africa for her to buy a pram for David.

When Dorothy became stronger, she paid visits to No. 11 and my Dad escorted her home. She would eventually walk miles and miles with David in his pram. Life for Dorothy was now falling into a pattern of coping with shortages of everything: food, clothing, and not least cash.

From time to time, a censored card would arrive from me. These consisted of three sentences and twenty-five words of our own composition. As each of these cards arrived, Dorothy would inform the *Burton Daily Mail*, and in this way all our friends would hear. On one occasion, a card came with a letter from an Irishman who had salvaged about ten from a plane which had crashed and set on fire in Southern Ireland. Despite Dorothy's efforts at the time to trace him, and mine after my return, we had no replies from our letters. Long after the war, in about 1988 when I had joined some FEPOW organizations, I learned that mine was among the first batch of cards to come to Britain, and the plane had left Gibraltar and was over Ireland in order to avoid German fighters when it crashed.

These facts do not appear much as the contents of over four years of Dorothy's life, which proves that it was little more than a daily chore of existence.

Dorothy, when she became well enough, started to play her violin again and was in a couple of orchestras, one of which was run by the Auxiliary Fire Service. It was when returning from one of these venues that Dorothy and her friend were harassed by a couple of American soldiers and so they decided to resign. But rather than lose their services, the fire service decided to provide transport, which was looked upon with disdain by a few dubious-minded people. Dorothy was still a member of May Clarke's Orchestra when I came home, and had the unique experience of playing at Burton Town Hall on both VE Day and VJ Day. The music was relayed into King Edward Place, where everyone was dancing. On VJ Day, Dorothy was presented with a bouquet and wishes for a speedy reunion with 'Jim'.

So there we were on that Armistice Sunday morning, having made our plans for the day. We set off to visit Uncle Len and Auntie Gladys in Shobnall Street, and again No. 11 and to take my first look at Burton in daylight.

The streets were empty, with no parked cars (or moving ones either) in those days, only a handful of people who made their way to church. Little did these people know as they passed a young couple with a little boy, what was going on in three bewildered minds.

David ran along happily enough and had already seemed to accept me, and I did not appear a stranger to him. This was due to his Mother having often talked to him of me, and I was certain that at this stage he knew more about me than I did of him.

Dorothy hung closely on my arm and talked non-stop, telling me anything she could of what had happened during my absence. I, of course, was only too pleased to listen, because this was just what I wished – the three of us together and all the world to enjoy.

For many weeks I was quite happy to listen and learn, plan for the future, and try to realize that I could do just what I wished, go where I wanted and simply enjoy being home. My silence was often not appreciated, and was taken as a sign of discontent, but this could not be further from the truth. However, over the coming weeks and months, Dorothy (who had been briefed by Welfare workers what to expect), with love, patience and at times some firmness, returned me to humanity. Many wives were not so loving and caring as Dorothy, and many marriages fell by the wayside, while many men did not fully return to life.

Anyway, we were almost at 147 Shobnall Street. It was less than 48 hours since we had docked at Southampton; so much had happened and I had already learned so much that it seemed I had been home for ages. No wonder that in my own mind I was becoming bewildered, but only I was aware of this and it was almost frightening me, yet I knew I had to get on with it or flounder.

As we entered the yard of 147, Uncle Len was just leaving his workshop, and up went his arms in disbelief at seeing us. In the house we went, and Aunty Gladys made such a fuss and asked so many questions. 'When did you come?' 'Didn't anyone know you were coming?' Uncle Len went to the kitchen and shed a few tears of joy (and I guess said a little prayer, knowing him), because Dorothy was his favourite niece. Although we only intended a brief initial visit, Aunty insisted we had a cup of tea while she talked at about a thousand words per minute. We thus fell behind schedule at our first fence!

Next, we made our way to No. 11 and were fortunate not to meet anyone we knew en route.

Once in No. 11, 'Big Jim' and Beatie from No. 10 came in to say 'welcome', and were thoughtful enough not to stay and encroach on our reunion too much. There was now a strange quietness and atmosphere of calmness. My sisters, who had turned from schoolgirls into young ladies, hardly knew what to say to me, hiding their shyness by entertaining David. My parents, who like everyone else would have liked to know what had happened to me over the last four years, had enough sense to know that was not the time to ask. They were quite satisfied that I was home and in fair enough shape. When our brief visit was about to end, my Mother said, 'Can you have a quick word with "Grandad" before you go?'

'Grandad' Fitzjohn, whom I have described earlier, was on his front doorstep when I went round, making sure he saw me before I left. I swear he almost ran when he was called. By the time we had shaken hands, the rest of the family from No. 13 had flooded in, and as they were all females you can imagine what a cackle was going on. I could only afford to stay a couple of minutes before rejoining Dorothy and David and making tracks to No. 78 for dinner. As we walked up the path to 78, all the neighbours started their greetings but we were home and not late for dinner. By now all the world knew that Jim was home!

In the afternoon we had planned to go for a walk around the Outwoods Rec. Dorothy's Mum asked us to pay a quick call on her great friend Mrs Richards, a couple of doors away. We sat and talked after dinner until it was too late for our walk, so we settled for a ten-minute visit to Mrs Richards, and then it was tea time.

It was decided that it was too late for David to walk to Blackpool Street, and as there were no Sunday buses, Dorothy and I would go on our own after tea. David would stay with his Grandma and Grandad and get to bed early as his sleep schedule had been disturbed.

We enjoyed our walk and were on our own again, chatting away, and we arrived at my Grandma's back door before we realized it.

My Grandma, like everyone else, did not know that I was home, and as she was about 80 years of age, we did not want to surprise her too much. It was custom to knock on the door and walk in; doors did not have to be locked after dark in those days. Dorothy knocked and went in first, calling, 'It's me, Dorothy, and I've got somebody to see you!' When Grandma saw me, she had a few tears, asked the same questions – 'When did you come?' etc. – and made such a fuss. We stayed about an hour, then made our way back to No. 78 by about ten o'clock. Then we had a quiet moment with Dorothy's Mum before we retired for the night. The first day was over; the most important contacts were made in the most hectic three days of my life.

On the Monday, people were back to work, shops were open and more people were on the streets. Now as we walked around, we were meeting friends and all of them steered the conversation into the same pattern. They all seemed to see me as some sort of hero, which I was not. I had only been in an unfortunate situation, and considered myself one of the more fortunate ones. They all wanted to know the worst side of an episode which I was determined to forget, and which I also had no intention of those close to me learning about. It was weeks before the pattern of these meetings changed, and inwardly I used to get quite heated about it. I would have little to say, and then my silence would upset the ones I was trying to protect – most of all Dorothy.

I knew I had to return to Cosford in early December, but had been promised that I would be home for Christmas; of course, Dorothy and I were looking forward to this – as was everyone else, but for us it was extra special.

After a couple of days, a poor old railway drayman arrived at 78A. Due to shortage of labour, he had been retained at work long after retirement age. He came to deliver the two overweight kit bags, which he could not lift off his horse-drawn dray.

With the help of a passer-by, I got them off the dray and up to the house by means of his sack-truck, whilst Dorothy's mum made him a cup of tea. I asked the old chap, 'Do you smoke?' 'When I get the chance,' he said. I gave him a tin of fifty Players cigarettes, and the happiness of that old chap I will never forget. Anyhow, we now had the two large bags of jam, fruit, etc. safely home to help our Christmas.

I went to visit my old workmates at Worthington's Brewery – where Worthington Walk and the car park now stand – and was warmly welcomed by everyone, particularly the older ones who had served in the First World War.

Time passed quickly, and I went back to Cosford. A few more medical tests were done and we were allocated in small groups to a PT corporal for exercises. Our corporal was Gill Merrick, who was the current Wolves and England goalkeeper. It didn't take us long to establish a routine — it was to a little pub about a couple of miles away, and the exercise was throwing darts at a board or shuffling cards or dominoes! About a week later, we were on our way home again until January.

Christmas was a homely affair, but due to rationing and austerity the big feasts and parties had not yet returned. Neither had a lot of the lads, including Uncle Lol. Nevertheless, it was a great Christmas all the same.

I travelled back and forth to Cosford, and had a spell in hospital there with malaria until I finally got demobilized on 1 March 1946, although I was on RAF pay (due to overdue leave etc.) until mid-July. I returned to work in mid-March.

From then, along with Dorothy, we had to start life as married and ordinary people, and see what life had in store for us.

Young Jim Banton pictured with his younger sister Winifred at thier Grandmothers house at No 2 Blackpool Street, Burton on Trent. This was taken in the mid 1920's when very few people owned a camera.

Ebenezer Banton - Royal Field Artillery WW1- served in Ireland, Galliopi , Mesopatania (Iraq) and India.

Jim Banton - far right, his cousin Ray Banton far left. Third from left on front row was Jim's best mate and best man Vic Reed. Fighter pilot in WW2, killed in action. 1937–38.

Dorothy (Jims future wife) with brother Lawrence (left) and neigbour Jack Hayes at 78a Victoria Crescent - The Masons Family home.

43 Alexandra Road , Blackpool - Boarding House during training -1940. Jim Banton back row far left. Fellow Burtonian Cyril Fletcher back row far right. WW1 vetran wearing medal ribbons 2nd left front row.

West Raynham rescue team - top left W. Clarke crash wagon driver. Top right F. Winter ambualnce driver and far right Jim Banton.

JB (right) in summer fatigues - 1942. Taken with J Milne a butcher in the RAF -
he never survived the camps

Group photo of the men who arrived by a Sunderland aircraft getting ready to start their journey home on board The Highland Monarch from Columbo. This is the first photo taken after their release. The hospital was the Hotel Mount Lavinia which is situated on a tropical beach. It is featured monemtarily in the film - Bridge over the river Kwai. Jim is second from the left in the front row. His close freind Jack Brown who is standing in the centre of the photo with the nurse on his left. This man saved Jim's life in the camps just by talking to him everyday and giving him the hope to survive. Out of all the photos these are the most poignant - Jim weighed 6st 4 lb

Home at last - first picture of the family together after Jim's return. A poignant photo as it shows a marked difference in him if compared with the photo on the front cover of the book. His face cannot hide the memories of recent years.

NEWS OF BURTON MEN.

Prisoners of Japanese.

Mrs. Banton, of 78a, Victoria Crescent, Burton, has received notification from the Air Ministry, that her husband Leading Aircraftman James Henry Banton, is a prisoner of war in Japanese hands.

In April, Mrs. Banton was informed that he must be regarded as missing. His whereabouts had been unknown since the evacuation of the Malaya, Java and Sumatra areas. He does not know that he has a 16 - months - old son, David.

Prior to joining up three years ago, L.A.C. Banton was employed at Messrs. Worthington and Co.'s brewery.

He is the only son of Mr. and Mrs. E. Banton, of 11, Victoria Street, Burton.

Burton Mail - Jim is missing.

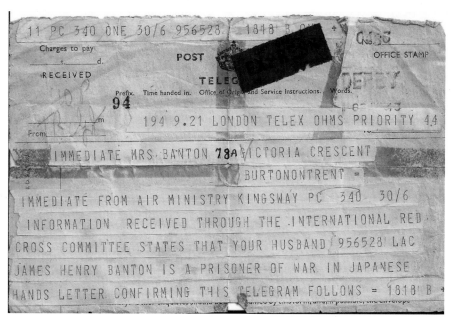

Official confirmation that Jim is a Japanese POW.

A BURTONIAN'S DIARY.

BY lucky chance, Mrs. D. J. Banton, of 78a, Victoria Crescent, has received news from her husband L.A.C. James H. Banton, from whom she has not heard since the fall of Singapore. Two months ago she had official intimation that he was a prisoner of war in Japanese hands in Java.

In her letter box on Saturday was a letter with an Eire postmark, signed Gerard O'Connor, which contained a dirty and damaged postcard written her from her husband in which he stated that he was in excellent health. Mr. O'Connor wrote: "This is a card which I found in the wreckage of a 'plane which crashed here. This card and about 10 more, escaped being burned, although thousands were burned. Hoping this will bring you good news, and trusting you will see your husband back again soon."

*   *   *

MRS. BANTON has sent a message of thanks to Mr. O'Connor. L.A.C. Banton is the only son of Mr. and Mrs. E. Banton, of 11, Victoria Street, and before the war he was employed by Messrs. Worthington and Co. He has a child born two months after the fall of Singapore, and whom he therefore has not seen.

*   *   *

Burton mail article and letter regarding his first message back home slavaged from a crashed aircraft.

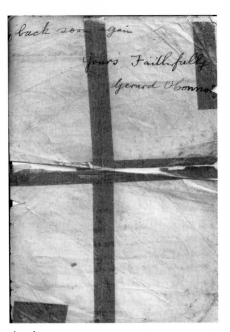

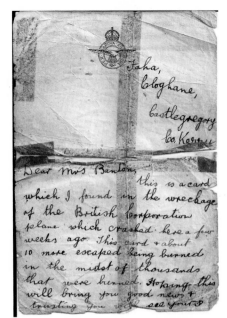

As above.

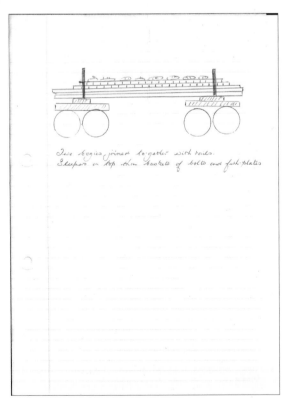

Jim's drawing to explain how the materials needed for the days work on the railway were assemblied ready to travel up the line.

This was Jims only possesion during his time in the camps and it kept this hidden throughout at great personal risk. Jims mother in law sent him this in 1940. It had a stainless steel mirror inside the sheath which rotted in the tropical climate. The theory was that you would put this in your breast pocket to protect your heart. The sheath also contanied the picture of Dorothy.

Dorothy with new born David - Jim saw him for the first time when he was nearly 4 years old.

Jim at the crease - keen cricketer. Taken in the garden of 11 Victoria Street.

The Banton Family - Back L-R - Ebenezer,Elsie (Mum & Dad), Winifred, Jim. Front Margaret and Kathleen. Before WW2.

A young Jim & Dorothy

Jim and dad Ebenezer a WW1 Galipolli veteran.

Jim promoted to foreman at Renold shows his family around his section on an Open Day. L-R – Jim, grandsons Adrian and Stephen, son in law Roy, grandaughter Karen, Daughter Jeanne, Dorothy, grandson Peter , daughter in law Jean and son David.

Burton Orient 1947 - Reformed in 1947 as a tribute to their lost colleague Vic Reed. Jim – far right.

Ex POW's Len Williams and Jim (right).

Christmas – 1990's Front L-R Dorothy & Jim. Middle - Jacqueline & Jeanne. Back - David & Keith.

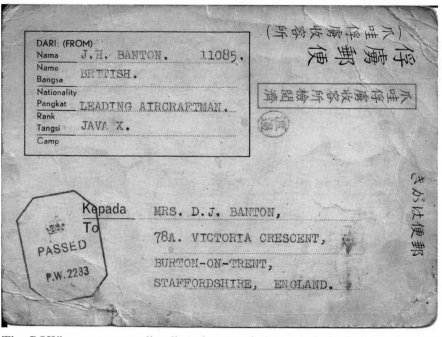

MY HEALTH IS EXCELLENT.

I AM CONSTANTLY THINKING OF YOU.   IT WILL BE
WONDERFUL WHEN WE MEET AGAIN.

GOODBYE.   GOD BLESS YOU.   I AM WAITING FOR YOUR
REPLY EARNESTLY.

GLAD YOU AND DAVID ALRIGHT.   GIVE MY LOVE TO
EVERYONE.   KEEP SMILING AND YOUR CHIN UP.
BETTER DAYS ARE AHEAD.

Jim Banton.

DARI: (FROM)

Nama	J.H. BANTON.	11085.
Name Bangsa	BRITISH.	
Nationality Pangkat	LEADING AIRCRAFTMAN.	
Rank Tangsi	JAVA X.	
Camp		

俘虜郵便
大阪俘虜收容所
大阪俘虜收容所檢閲済

さがは便郵

PASSED
P.W. 2233

Kepada
To

MRS. D.J. BANTON,

78A. VICTORIA CRESCENT,

BURTON-ON-TRENT,

STAFFORDSHIRE,   ENGLAND.

The POW's were eventually allowed to send these cards back home however they did not receive and letters form home during their time in the camps. They were allowed to choose from set phrases and allowed to add 20 words of thier own. Dorothy received only 6 of these cards in the 4 years Jim was away.

Photo and caption by Tim Love, circa late 1990s, used with permission. Haji RAMLI. He told me he was a young boy when then Japanese forced local Romusha to build the railway. He worked on the railway. He told me that many Romusha were thrown into the river, often alive, when they were too ill to work. Subsequently, locals wouldn't drink from the river. He tells me many thousands died here.

Photo and caption by Tim Love, circa late 1990s, used with permission. Haji SAIDI, again he was forced to work on the railway as a youngster. He said he buried Dutch and possibly Allied PoW's.

Photo and caption by Tim Love, circa late 1990s, used with permission. A concrete structure/support for a bridge that I found. Amazing that it still exists.

Photo and caption by Tim Love, circa late 1990s, used with permission. Abandoned locomotive found in the middle of the jungle.

Chapter 7

The Harsh Reality

After months of consoling myself with the thought that 'one day it will all be over' and dreaming of a life of absolute bliss, now came the harsh reality of life.

Although during the war I had switched from a happy, sport-loving teenager to a family man – an immense change in lifestyle – this was the change which I had longed for. It was due to the circumstances that it now appeared to have happened overnight, and somehow the interlude seemed to me not to have existed. All that now mattered to me was that I was there with Dorothy and David, and together we were looking forward to many happy years of life.

But such dreams now turned to hard facts. Lawrence had returned home, and the already overcrowded situation at 78A had become worse. With only two bedrooms, Lawrence had to sleep downstairs. I always felt that it was me who had brought this situation about, but despite all the inconveniences and discomfort it caused, we all lived in complete harmony. This was once again testimony to the love of Dorothy's parents.

Consequently, the first priority was to find somewhere to live. However, there was an acute housing shortage; hundreds of couples were in the same hopeless situation as ourselves.

With Lawrence being older than Dorothy by some six years, and her parents older than my own, Dorothy had not enjoyed the same lifestyle as a child and teenager that I had. She had lived as an only child, with all the love and over-protection which that brings. It was not surprizing that she loved to be at No. 11, where all my friends and sisters' friends gathered and wandered in and out at will. As a result of this, when it was realized that we thought enough of each other to talk about our future, Dorothy made it quite clear that, God willing, she intended to have more family.

Once my RAF pay ceased, the cash situation reared its head. Due to shortages of grain and other materials, the production of beer was restricted. As there was no overtime, the basic rate was only just enough for essentials. I had some £800 in a Post Office book, which was my four years' RAF pay and which we had earmarked for furniture etc. (when and if it became available).

After a few weeks back at work, an over-age man retired and I was given his job in Internal Traffic. The wage was only a few shillings per week more, but it was unusual for a man of my tender years to have this position, as quite a lot of responsibility went with it. The brewery had no lorries and everything was moved, even internally, by rail. I had to ensure that sufficient empty wagons were available to dispatch the ale, supply the brewery with malt, hops, sugar, clean casks and coal, transfer ale from the brewery to ale stores around the town and supply movement to and from maltings. In short, whatever wanted moving, I had to make sure it moved at the right time. I thoroughly enjoyed this job, but the money fell short of what I wanted to achieve.

I applied for a company house, but there was no chance, well not until one day my boss sent for me and gave me the keys to a house. He told me to go and have a look at it straight away. It was in Nunnerley's Yard and was approached via a little slip road from Bridge Street (Nunnerley House is still there), and stood on what is now the car park behind the Bargates Centre. Surrounded by the dilapidated ruins of Salt's Brewery, it looked, to say the least, uninviting. When I got inside, I could not believe that someone had been living in it. I had a quick look around, and was soon on my way back to my boss. When I told him what I had seen, he could not believe me. However, he returned the key to the property people and passed on my comments. The next day I had to go and see Mr C.A. Ball, the chairman and MD of Worthington's. He wanted to know why I had refused the house, and was very kind to me and sympathetic to the fact that I had been a FEPOW. As a result of what I told him, he called for a report on the house and it was demolished as beyond repair. Sometime later, Mr Ball sent for me again and offered me the tenancy of the Essex Arms in Victoria Street – now a dwelling house about halfway between Victoria Road and Dallow Street on the Derby Street side. I decided that life in a pub was not what I wanted for Dorothy and not a fit place to bring up children, and although the terms were tilted very favourably to my advantage, I declined. Furthermore, by this time we had other irons in the fire.

A neighbour of 78A was Mr A. Whetton, a councillor and ex-mayor of Burton, who was on the Housing Committee. He was well aware of the situation which we were in, and was keeping us in his mind.

It was during this period that we were invited to a couple of 'Welcome Home' parties. One was held for the lads around Victoria Street in the schoolroom of Victoria Street Chapel. The remains of this room are now used as a repair garage, although the chapel which stood in front of it is long since demolished. It stood opposite Edward Street and the Duke of York public house. A larger affair was held at the Town Hall and was for all ex-PoWs, those held by both the Germans and Japanese. It was organized by a committee which had been sending parcels to PoWs throughout the war. (No parcels of any description arrived for FEPOWs.) Gordon Manners, a director of Worthington's Brewery, had been a PoW in Germany, and therefore there was an adequate supply of beer and a good meal. Buses were laid on to collect and return everyone and their wives.

A few things were also becoming available if you happened to be lucky enough to be on the scene when they appeared. One such capture we had was a laundry wringer with rubber rollers, which replaced a huge cast-iron monstrosity with wooden rollers. The effort saved by this article was like the eighth wonder of the world to Dorothy's Mum, and we were fortunate enough to get a second one which we gave to her as a small appreciation of all her help.

In December 1946 came the realization of our dream for a house. Some prefabricated homes had been erected on a site between Harper Avenue and Rolleston Road, the concrete roads for which had been laid by Italian PoWs. We had the keys to No. 3 St Chad's Road. It was a foggy Friday night when Dorothy and I set off down Harper Avenue on our bikes to find our new house. There were no street lamps up, and with the fog we saw no street names, so we went right round the estate looking for a house with No. 3 on it and trying our key in the door – eventually with success. We retraced our tracks round to the avenue and back home to report on what little we could see by the light of our cycle lamps.

On the Saturday morning, we were off again to await the gas and electricity people to connect the services. Those bungalows were fantastic, with two good bedrooms, hall, bathroom, lounge and a dream of a kitchen with hot and cold water, gas cooker and even a fridge and wash boiler all fitted. Maybe it appears no great deal nowadays, but in 1946 it was the first time either Dorothy or I had enjoyed a house with the luxury of a bathroom, let alone a fridge. These things only belonged to the very rich folk. Furthermore, both bedrooms were well equipped with fitted wardrobes.

Now it was all systems go. Aunty Gladys and Dorothy's Mum were in on the act, making curtains from bed sheets and dying them in order to save the ration dockets for some smart front curtains and other essentials. We had bought a bedroom suite and a dining-room suite, which were stored at the home of our friends the Fletchers in Waterloo Street. The three-piece suite which Dorothy had bought during the war had to be got out via the bedroom window. All our plans came to fruition, and we were installed in our new home a fortnight before Christmas.

Summer 1947 saw many changes. At work there was a vacancy for a petrol-loco driver, and as it carried the highest rate of pay at the brewery and the chance of a small amount of overtime, I applied for it and was successful. Although it was against the advice of my boss, the money was the attraction.

At home I was busy converting a rough piece of field into a garden. I cut some turf from spare land nearby and laid us a lawn, and the vegetable section yielded fantastic crops – mushrooms even grew between the rows.

By midsummer, we three were set to become four – the old saying 'new house, new baby' had come true. This news did not go down well with Dorothy's Mother, simply because she feared that Dorothy would be ill again, as she was with David. I was not her favourite for a long time, and unfortunately she was right.

On a Saturday in October, Dorothy was in town with her mum and was taken ill with what appeared to be the flu, and had to hail a taxi to come home. At tea time, Dorothy was much worse and I had to send for the doctor. A doctor we did not previously know came (Dr Dutton), and he said I was to meet him at Bridge Street surgery on Sunday morning with samples from Dorothy. After performing the tests, he said Dorothy was to go into hospital. She went on to Ward 7 (the maternity ward) at New Street Infirmary.

As I visited Dorothy each day, I was sure that she was getting worse. When I went on the following Saturday evening, her room was all sealed off with tape around the doors. I went to the office and a nurse said that Dorothy was now on Ward 5, but would not say why. On Ward 5, a nurse was on duty and again would not say what the trouble was. I went in to see Dorothy; her face was black and she was half-conscious, saying, 'Let me die!'

I couldn't get any information from the nurse, and as I left the hospital I called at the lodge to ask if I could use the phone. The lady on duty lived opposite Dorothy's Mum and Dad, and she advised me to ring from the call box in the street. I did, but Dr Brewer, who had now returned from holiday, was out. His wife said, 'Call again at 9 o'clock.' This I did, and he asked me what I suspected. I guessed meningitis, but he said, 'No, I'm afraid she has poliomyelitis – go home, have a stiff whisky and get some sleep.' The news was as shattering to Dorothy's and my parents as it was to me. As for sleep – I ask you? David was staying with Dorothy's Mum, and I spent the night mostly walking round the streets with our faithful dog, Roger, as company.

There was no change in Dorothy's condition on Sunday, and on Monday morning I went to see Dr Brewer at his surgery. He told me that they had drawn the fluid from Dorothy's spine. If they had done this at precisely the correct time, all would be well – too soon or too late, and it would be another story. Only the next few days would tell. They were a long few days, but they had done a wonderful job. Dr Dutton had made a good early diagnosis! Dorothy began to get better. I will never forget when I first saw her walking around home. Poor Dorothy: she had lost so much weight, could hardly stand up straight and her legs were no thicker than pencils. She smiled at me and said, 'Don't worry, duck! I won't always look such a mess – I'll get better!'

Although Dorothy's mum could not find it in herself to accept me at the time, I did not retaliate as I could understand her feelings, and between us we looked after Dorothy and protected her through the winter.

In the following February, Dorothy returned to Ward 7 and Jeanne was born well and safely on the 8th. She was a beautiful little girl with a mop of thick, black curly hair. On the day I fetched Dorothy and Jeanne from hospital, I had to wait while the sister showed Jeanne off to all the wards. She had set Jeanne's hair as if it had been permed – Jeanne still curses the curls!

As we left the hospital, my Father got out of an ambulance which was taking my Uncle Bill in with pneumonia – he died later that day.

Once Dorothy and Jeanne were safely home and well, I became her Mum's favourite son-in-law again and stayed so until Jacqueline was due on the scene.

The winter of 1947 had been a particularly hard one. Not only had it been severe, but also prolonged. The power stations were antiquated and unable to cope, which resulted in power cuts becoming a way of life. Coal was rationed to gas works and factories, and very difficult to get for domestic use. I was working at ale stores in Wetmore Road, and spent my dinner hour queuing for sacks of coke[1] which I would push home on the crossbar of my bike. The roads, for weeks, were frozen in solid ruts, and were so compacted they became black. I wondered if they would ever thaw out. Everyone became like circus stars on bicycles and developed the skill of riding sideways as if that was how you should ride.

We were quite a happy family during the summer of 1948. Dorothy really enjoyed living in the 'prefab', and the garden was in good order. The only problem on the horizon now was that we only had two bedrooms, and with two children of opposite sex this was not permitted by the local authorities. Neither Dorothy nor I wished to live in Stapenhill or Winshill, where all the house building was taking place. Out of the blue, we learned that the council was to build some three-bedroom houses off Rolleston Road. We soon applied for one of these houses and watched anxiously as they were built.

Phil Smith and I had during the year decided that we would like to resurrect Burton Orient FC as a tribute to our pal Vic Reed, who worked so hard for the club until the war intervened. We rounded up nine others and got this off the ground after overcoming many difficulties. We had no kit, our goal posts had been 'adopted' by Ind Coope FC, the school room at St Margaret's church had become derelict and we could find nowhere to change. As a last resort, I approached the Education Officer, Mr Blake, and after much deliberation and several meetings, we were granted use of the cloakroom in Casey Lane of Grange Street School. We were admitted to the Burton FA, and our first match was at Rangemore. There being no buses, we hired a small coach, each one paying his fare and off we went. We spent the outward journey introducing the players to each other, and at least we were in business.

The houses being built off Rolleston Road were nearing completion and we had been assured that we would have one. I arrived home from work around five o'clock on a Friday evening in December to learn that Dorothy had been given the keys to No. 7 St Andrew's Drive. The fly in the ointment was that we had to move in over the weekend and hand in the keys for 3 St Chad's Road at 10am on the following Monday.

---

[1] Gas at this time was produced by local council-run works, and coke was a by-product. Gas works produced good revenue to support local rates, but when centralised the gas was bought from Derby and eventually 'natural gas' arrived.

Fortunately, it was a day when Orient had no match. We hired a van, and with help from Lawrence and a few of the lads, we made it.

Again it was a fortnight prior to Christmas when we moved in, the weather was foul, no pavements had been laid and the house was surrounded by a sea of muddy red clay. I remember that as we carried the piano across the front, someone lost a shoe, and when we stood the piano down while the shoe was retrieved, the piano sank about three inches into the mud. Eventually we had the furniture in and the gas fitters and electricity people out. Mud had been tramped all over the house and our clothes were in sacks, but we didn't even doubt whether it was worth the trouble. Dorothy and her mother produced cups of tea and something to eat while we erected the beds, and with a good fire in the grate, things began to look a little more hopeful. Anyway, up until now we have lived here for over forty years, so it must have been right!

The summer of 1949 was a busy time for me. The back garden was 3ft higher than the ground floor of the house, and only 1 yard for scaffolding had been cleared. In order to make a back garden (now called a patio), I spent my spare time taking the excess soil away by wheelbarrow and tipping it into the nearest field. I had also now become involved in decorating. I had done some for Dorothy's parents, and was asked by someone who saw it to do likewise for them, as materials were now becoming available, but labour wasn't. This became quite a godsend to us, as it eased our budget problems. At one stage I had a whole year's bookings. Often I would paper one room on Saturday and another on Sunday.

Whilst Dorothy and I had been involved in the hectic past couple of years with all these problems of our own, other events were carrying on their day-to-day procedures.

On Boxing Day 1947, Margaret had married Cyril at St Paul's Church, and in May 1948, Kathleen had married his friend from the RAF, Bert. Margaret and Kathleen had met the two RAF lads at a Town Hall dance, and had now become Mrs Burton and Mrs Renton.

During 1949, my Grandmother Mrs Chambers died at the age of 82. Formerly Mrs Key, she was the only one of my grandparents whom I knew.

In July of 1949, Lawrence married Sylvia in Cardiff and Dorothy went to act as bridesmaid. Dorothy's Father had been ill, and as he was not well enough to go, her Mother tended for David and Jeanne while we went.

From this time on, it seemed that we would make one step forward and one step backwards. We were getting our house in some sort of shape, as I was earning a little from my sideline and also getting a little overtime at the brewery.

My mother's hip had deteriorated. At Burton we now had a new orthopaedic surgeon, Mr Davis, and he decided to fit a plastic hip for her. This was one of the first operations of its kind, and was successful in as much as it saved many years of pain and conserved her restricted mobility for perhaps ten years or so. It was only due to the delay in the availability of the treatment that the distortion of her legs prevented a complete recovery. Today, these operations are routine and have a very high success rate.

I had called in to see my folks at No. 11 one evening to enquire how Margaret was, as she had just given birth to her second child. Cyril came in from his visit to the hospital and he could not speak; he simply handed a letter from Margaret to my Mother. As Cyril undressed Brian for bed, the letter was passed round and we learned that Glenys had been born with spina bifida – thus another happy event was overtaken by sadness. Glenys lived and was loved for many years, but was finally taken ill on Boxing Day (Cyril and Margaret's wedding anniversary) and died a couple of days later.

It was in 1951 that I decorated a house in Branston Road from top to bottom, and with the proceeds No. 7 became about the first house in St Andrew's Drive with a TV set. This was in the days before most TVs came from Japan, when they were made by Bush, GEC, Ferguson, HMV and others. We had a GEC. It was a constant source of trouble, and after two years was replaced, free of charge, by a much-improved model which gave good service until we replaced it when ITV came into being. We later became the first on the scene with a colour TV.

The year 1952 was one of several highlights, again following the pattern of 'win one, lose one'. King George VI had died in 1951, all TV and radio was silenced, and I joked with Dorothy that as there was only one entertainment available, a lot of trouble could follow! So it came to be that in 1952 we learned that our family was to increase in size. It also came to be that the same applied to four or five other families in the neighbourhood.

It was understandable that Dorothy's Mum became worried once again, although the doctors assured us that the two previous illnesses were not caused by the pregnancy.

During Dorothy's pregnancy this time, she kept good health and we had a 'TV Party' at No. 7 to celebrate the Coronation of Elizabeth II and Prince Philip. We entertained Dorothy's Mum and Dad, Uncle

Jim, Aunty Gladys and John Smith (who lived with Len and Gladys). The TV coverage was on all day long and we organized meals around the highlights. It was the first time the world had been able to see such a spectacle. A similar party took place at No. 11 and any house which had a TV set.

It was about this time that my Father's health began to deteriorate, and he had long spells off work with bronchial problems and pneumonia.

In 1950, David had a lump on his thigh which we thought was brought on with the start of the football season. However, as there was no sign of it subsiding, Dorothy took him along to the doctor. X-rays showed that he had a spur growing from his thigh. Mr Davis, the surgeon, said if this was not removed it would grow into the muscle and lock his leg permanently stiff. This was a particular blow to David as he had just settled in to the Grammar School (in Bond Street).

When the operation was performed, it was late in Dorothy's pregnancy and as soon as it was over I went out from work to see David. In the corridor at the 'General', I met Mr Davis, who asked me where I was going and assured me that David would be fine. After some weeks of physio and wearing a leg-iron, all was well and David has had no further trouble – so thanks a second time, Mr Davis.

Before David's leg had recovered, he had a second sister to cope with. Dorothy had kept well this time, and I came home for dinner on 24 October to find sprouts and potatoes etc. simmering away gently on the stove but no sign of Dorothy. After a few minutes, I went to see 'Aunty Joyce' Holiday at No. 5 to discover that Dorothy had called an ambulance and gone to hospital; Jeanne was at No 5. On my way back to work, I took Jeanne to Dorothy's Mother. I phoned the hospital from work during the afternoon, and left early to prepare to visit Dorothy in the evening. As I made my way to 78A ready to go to the hospital, I phoned from the call box at Horninglow Post Office to enquire of Dorothy. A nurse said, 'Wait a minute, I'll see.' A few seconds later she told me, 'Mrs Banton has just had her baby, OK.'' 'What have we got?' I asked. As it had only just happened, the nurse was not able to say, but she said I could visit in an hour's time. When I told Dorothy's Mum but could not say whether it was boy or girl, she hit the roof. 'Don't you care at all?' she said, and was none too pleased with my explanation. However, all was well when after my visit I called in to say that we had a lovely fair-haired Jacqueline. We had many laughs later. Dorothy's Mum laughed about it herself, and she was quite proud of the one she called her 'Dolly Varden'.

The situation at the brewery was changing and I was working a lot of overtime. As well as the extra trade, a lot of maintenance had been neglected during the war and most weekends some plate-laying was done. As the only other diesel driver was older, he didn't care for weekend work so I had the benefit. This meant that I had to abandon my spare time work, as the work at the brewery was better paid and fewer hours. Although we were now better off financially, it meant that Dorothy had to cope with three children and her housework, and she even spent a lot of time on the garden.

By the time 1955 came along, my Father was getting more poorly. He had a serious bout of pneumonia and went to Ind Coope's convalescent home at Bournemouth for a while, and after a long lay-off returned to work as cabin man for the coopers. I called to see him late one night on my way home from work and he was tormenting my Mother and Kath (who was living there), singing 'Enjoy yourself, it's later than you think'. At about eight o'clock the following morning, I was working at the ale stores in Wetmore Road when I saw my cousin Bill walking up the yard. Before I got off the engine, I guessed it was about my Dad. He had died suddenly at work. I made my way to No. 11, from where I was taken by police car to the mortuary to identify my Father. On my way to No. 11, I had met David on his way to school and had told him what had happened, and I was already regretting having been so thoughtless as to do that. Anyhow, as I pulled up at home in the police car, Dorothy saw me as she was preparing to go into town. Although we had not yet confided in anyone, Dorothy and I were certain that we were to have another addition to our family and I had given her some money to treat herself – another little joy was accompanied with sorrow.

Kath and Bert were living with my Mother, so that was a blessing. However, Dorothy's Mother was very poorly and after some harsh words from Dorothy, the doctor had her Mum admitted to hospital. By this time she was in a very serious condition with pneumonia, and the hospital was not all pleased about the delay which had occurred. When eventually Mum was due for discharge, we brought her to No. 7 and took care of her and Dad.

During the winter, Dorothy's Dad had a modern grate installed at 78A, knocked the old brick copper out of the kitchen and replaced it with a gas boiler. I decorated from top to bottom, and when Mum was fit to return in the spring, we had vases of daffodils in the house and the sun shone to set the scene. When Mum walked in, she shed a few tears of joy and kept walking around, ignoring Dorothy's request to sit and have a cup of tea.

Dorothy and I are forever thankful that we were in a position to do this for her parents. It was as if someone in higher places had worked it all out for us. Not only had our financial situation begun to ease a little, but also I was able to find a few spare hours in which to do the work. Although her Mum's health gradually began to deteriorate, she did have some ten years or more to enjoy those few improvements to the home.

Chapter 8

One Step Forward, One Step Back

Dorothy and I had by now come to accept the fact that we were destined to win one and lose one as we proceeded along what is known as 'The highway of life'.

In 1956, in the early hours of 2 March – the day after her birthday – Dorothy went into labour. I called an ambulance, and in a blinding snowstorm off we went to St Modwen's Nursing Home in Union Street. Upon arrival, a nurse answered the door, took Dorothy's hand, took the case out of mine and said, 'Thank you. Good morning!' – and closed the door. The ambulance went off, and I had a long early-morning walk home in a freezing blizzard.

Keith was born safely, and all was well in our world again – for a little while. When Keith was only a few months old, Jeanne became ill and had to be admitted to the Children's Hospital in Birmingham. Once again our joy was replaced with worry and problems.

As Jeanne became more ill, Dorothy of course wanted to see her every day; for that matter so did I, but someone had to pay the fares and I had to go to work. Thankfully, David was by now old enough to not need complete attention, and Dorothy's Mum was able to cope with Jacqueline and Keith during the afternoons whilst Dorothy travelled alone to Birmingham. I could go at weekends if I was not at work.

In the autumn, Jeanne was well enough for convalescence and was moved to Great Malvern in Worcestershire. Because of the cost incurred and the fact that it was a twelve-hour trip there and back, it was now only possible for one visit per week on a Sunday. Dorothy would have a taxi to take the children to her Mother's at 78A and then her to the station. She would travel to Birmingham and walk from the Midland Station across to Snowhill, and on to Malvern Link station.

The hospital had no shelter anywhere around, and all through the winter, whether it rained or snowed, Dorothy would have to wait outside for visiting time. Then she had to make the return journey, which due to maintenance work on the line meant that it was always around 9pm when she arrived home – a twelve-hour day for a one-hour visit.

In order to finance this, I had got myself a Sunday job in the maltings in Wetmore Road (which is still there). I would finish around midday and was able to take the children home to relieve Dorothy's Mum. I could get them off to bed and have a good fire and a meal ready for Dorothy's return. I would take an occasional Sunday off to go with Dorothy. This could not happen often due to the finances and the extra burden on Dorothy's parents.

It was during my work in the maltings that I pulled off the wages scoop of all times – much to the displeasure of my own boss. I worked all day on Good Friday – ten hours at double time plus a day's holiday pay – and then five hours' double time on Saturday, a total of thirty-eight hours' pay for a day and a half.

The new week started on Sunday, and I worked again in the maltings at double time – sixteen hours' pay.

On Easter Monday I was required on my own job at 8am. I was also asked to work in the maltings, and when I had to turn it down to give my own work preference, the foreman said we could start at 5am and finish at 7.30am, so I was in. Under the maltings agreement, I got a day's holiday pay – eight hours and a full day's pay at double time, sixteen hours, which added up to twenty-four hours' pay for two-and-a-half hours' work. I then went to my own job from 8am to 4pm, and got paid a day's holiday pay at eight hours plus eight hours at double time – sixteen hours – for a total of another twenty-four hours. Thus, by Monday at 4pm I had sixty-four hours' pay on my card (a normal week was forty hours).

Jeanne came home in the spring, and life then settled into a more peaceful routine. I was able to do plenty of overtime, and all but Keith were at school. Dorothy, who had a little more time to spare, would visit her Mum. Often, as I was on my way back to work after dinner, I would meet her Mum walking as upright as a guardsman, her gloves and handbag swinging, hat at a jaunty angle and all the air of a duchess, on her way to No. 7.

We were now having a little more prosperity and things went much better for us for a couple of years. So it was that in 1959 we decided that we could afford to have a car, and we bought a Mk 1 Ford Consul, registration VVO 326.

Thus equipped, we had our first holiday at Trussville Holiday Camp at Mablethorpe in Lincolnshire. We spent a day at Grimsby to see the fishing fleet, and had a wonderful fish and chips lunch which Dorothy and I still talk of. At the end of the week, Dorothy and Jeanne had become ill and we came home in a hurry. The next year we went to a farmhouse at Porth in Wales – a beautiful place, but we came home on the Wednesday due to incessant rain.

By now Dorothy was doing evening work on the maternity ward at the Andressey Hospital, and at an annual party we decided that it was time we learned how to dance. To everyone's amazement, we took ourselves to Millicent Simmonds in Uxbridge Street, where Roy and Dorothy Moxon were the teachers. We walked in to find less than a dozen learners, and I asked, 'How do we join?' Roy Moxon said, 'Hang your coat up and join in!' This was one of the best moves we ever made, because we have enjoyed – and still do enjoy – many happy hours and occasions as a result. The third generation of our family still visit what is now Moxons, our grandson Adrian being an instructor.

Now that we had the car, we decided that we would like to take Dorothy's Mum and Dad to Wildboarclough. It was where her Dad came from and where her Mum met him whilst she was cook for Lord Derby. Dorothy's Grandad worked on the woodwork during the building of the church there, where her Mum and Dad were married.

We decided to reconnoitre the place first, and set off one Sunday afternoon. As we made our way over the moors and along a seemingly endless lane, we encountered a rainstorm of monsoon proportions. We asked a couple of half-drowned, bedraggled boy scouts, 'Where is Wildboarclough please?' 'This is it,' they said. Dorothy and I concluded that it was not the nice place which her Dad had led us to believe – but at least we knew where it was.

When we told her Mum and Dad that we would like to take them on the following Sunday, they were highly delighted. Her Dad kept telling us that the car would not take us up some of the hills, and we just laughed.

Off we went on the following Sunday, with enough food to sustain a month's safari. The weather was glorious, we had a picnic among the sheep on the moors, and Dorothy's Dad was pleased to show us the Cat and Fiddle pub high up on the top – and relate a few tales of his youthful activities!

From here, her Dad became navigator, and into narrow lanes we went. 'Turn right here!' he said. The lane was just wide enough to take the car, and around the corner the road rose up at about one-in-two. No way could we get up there with us all in the car, and her Dad laughed about that until his dying day. All except Dorothy's Mum and I had to walk up.

We arrived at 'The Clough', and no sooner had we stopped to have a look round when an elderly gentleman came from one of the cottages to ask if we required help. As I told him of the purpose of our visit, Dad came round from the other side of the car and carried on the story.

He asked if any of the 'old uns' were still alive, and was told, 'Aye – old Bill Sykes in the end cottage.' At this, the gentleman opened the door of another cottage, called out for a lady who was the daughter of Bill Sykes and explained to her who we were. We followed her into the end cottage, where although it was a boiling hot summer day, there sat Bill Sykes, wearing a thick woollen jumper, in front of a fire of about half a hundredweight of coal! He turned around and said, 'It's Jack Mason!', recognizing him after forty years. Dorothy's Dad had learned his trade from Bill many years ago.

After declining the offer of tea, we were directed to a farmer and his family to renew another acquaintance. Mum and Dad went to the door and were greeted as long-lost friends, and before I had put the car safe and joined them the table was being laden with loads of homemade produce and we had no option but to stay for tea this time – and very enjoyable it was too.

Before we left 'The Clough', we called on a cottage and visited one of the Gee family, in-laws of Aunty Rosa, and paid a visit to the church. Inside the church was immaculate, all the brass shone, a blue carpet covered the aisle and the altar was loaded with flowers. We have often visited this church since, and have always found it just as spick and span. A plaque on the wall bears the name of Dorothy's Dad and her uncle, and of a couple of the Gee family.

Dad was rightly proud to show us around this church, and Mum took us without hesitation to the grave of his Mother, where she laid some flowers.

It was late in the evening when we arrived back at 78A, and although we paid further visits before Mum's health began to fail, this first visit was the one which was always talked about. Dorothy and I have always been grateful that we had the opportunity to do this little favour, and to think that such small effort brought so much joy and happy memories to her Mum and Dad.

The next few years we had a more settled life pattern: children going to school, David was at work – although he was constantly changing jobs – and Dorothy and I were both at work. We were also having a little social life. We had the car, which enabled us to get out and about, and we had learned to dance, which brought us into contact with a new circle of friends.

In 1963, David became 21 and we had quite a good party which was held in St John's Church Hall. A few weeks later, however, we were back into the less happy events. David decided to leave home, and he was only just recovering from a serious eye operation which had worried us for some time. Once again, one highlight and one lowlight was par for the course. It was not long before he met Jean and became married. Although the marriage lasted some years and two sons, Stephen and Peter, were born, it was never completely happy and eventually they were to part.

A further worry at this time was my future at the brewery. The railways were being closed down and the brewing industry was being modernized on a massive scale. I was far from happy with the way the new jobs were being allocated, and was considering looking to work elsewhere.

The months of living under the cloud of uncertainty became unbearable, and I was not the easiest of people to live with. Dorothy, although obviously worried as much as I was, always put on a brave face and encouraged me to look on the bright side.

The winter of 1964 was a terrible one in all aspects. The weather was atrocious and I was working abnormal hours: starting at 5.30am and often working until 9pm and 10pm, in such weather and with little prospect for the future.

The deciding factor came when I was working barley trains to and from Shobnall to all parts of Burton. The snow was freezing in the tracks and we had to use the steam jet from the engine to thaw it out. While we worked on one side, the other side froze again and we had to thaw our way out again. It was so cold we had to burn cotton waste to thaw out the balance-pipes on the loco in order to get water into its boiler.

On one occasion at No. 8 maltings at Shobnall (almost at Branston), it was 11.30pm and we had a train of malt for the next day's brewing. The shunter went to a cottage nearby and mashed a can of tea, and we were ready to come back to Burton. I could not move the train and the shunter went to investigate, only to discover that one van had walked off the rail on the impacted frozen snow. We had no alternative but to leave the load there, but the following day the boss said we should have called out the plate-layers, had the van re-railed and delivered our train. As it was, I had left work at 12.20am, having started at 5.30am the previous day. Thus was the attitude of a man who sat in a heated office from 9am to 5pm.

Consequently, early in 1965, Dorothy asked if there were any vacancies at Renold Chains and I was offered an interview. I called on my way back to work one lunchtime and was offered a job as a machine operator. Dorothy was dubious as to whether or not I should accept this, as it was a complete contrast to what I was used to, but I was so fed up with what was happening at the brewery and the long hours I was working that I decided to accept. Much of the overtime I was working was taken in tax, our social life was non-existent and family life was suffering, so I thought that a few pounds per week were worth sacrificing. Also, I was mindful of the fact that very soon a lot more people would be forced to look for other jobs, and as I was 45 years old I may find it difficult to change later.

On the Wednesday of the first week, I was called into the foreman's office and offered a job as storeman – more money and the first of what was to be several fairly rapid promotions.

We had barely settled into our new routine, and I was working alternate fortnightly shifts of days and nights for the first time in my life, when we had an unexpected wedding on our hands. Jeanne, who was an apprentice hairdresser, was married in November at St John's Church. This has proved to be a happy marriage, and Roy and Jeanne have been blessed with Adrian and Karen.

I quite enjoyed my first Christmas at Renold, for many reasons. For the first time in my working life, I did not have to work excessive overtime prior to and after the holiday, neither did I have to go to work on Boxing Day. I was able to help Dorothy shop for presents and take part in the festive preparations, and I was not too tired to enjoy them when the festivities came. Further, each section at Renold held its shop-floor fuddle (a buffet where everyone brought some food and drink) and most sections held a dinner-dance; our section went to the Stanhope at Bretby.

Sadly, Dorothy's Mother was failing in health and was now completely blind. It was sad to see such a proud and grand old lady in such suffering but, true to her own standards, not once complaining and still concerning herself with the welfare of all her family. It was in March when Dorothy was called from the factory to learn that her Mother had passed away in her sleep at the age of 81.

July of 1966 of course brought our Silver Wedding. We held a family party at home and had many presents. As for Dorothy and myself, we were just happy to have reached this landmark.

By now I had settled down alright at Renold, and Dorothy's Dad had gone to live with Lawrence and Sylvia at No. 12 – he had appointed himself as resident hedge-trimmer to the neighbourhood. Hedge trimming was always one of his pleasures, and everyone was pleased to allow him to indulge in it. When he tired of this, he would let himself into No. 7 and indulge in his other hobby – the horseracing on television. He had the house to himself, and with his pipe of tobacco and his horses, he was content with life – as

content as one can be after losing one's partner of over 50 years. After a
short illness, Dad passed away in November 1968.

The chairman of Renold's shop stewards had died suddenly, and
simply because I had asked awkward questions at what few meetings
I had attended, I was cajoled into taking the job of secretary. As this was
a negotiating position and I had not been on the committee previously,
I must have been mad. After about a year of this, I realized that I was back
to square one in as much as all my spare time was spoken for and I had
adopted worries which I did not really want. At the AGM I decided enough
was enough and resigned from the post.

By now Jacqueline was at work, but alas her long-time ambition to become
a policewoman was thwarted due to her being just short of the minimum
height required. This minimum has since been reduced. Keith was now
our only one still at school.

At work I became a charge hand, and on the political front Ted Heath's
government introduced new employment regulations. Because of the
strict but delicate issues involved in this and the way it conflicted with
our agreed constitution with the company, a large proportion of the shop
floor and the Stewards Committee asked me to become chairman and see
this issue through the procedures.

As at home we were having a peaceful and enjoyable passage of our
lifetime, I was far from keen to do this. However, as pressure was kept
up and Dorothy had no objections, I decided I would do it. Never before
had a charge hand taken an official position, due to a possible conflict
of loyalties – to management or members – and the constitution did not
disallow this. Having sorted out the legalities of the situation, I became
chairman. Burton was the first Renold establishment to negotiate the
implications of the new Act, so all eyes were on us and the company
brought down Mr Garlick as senior director to take the chair. I am glad
to say that after a long and tense discussion, we came to an agreement on
all the major issues at our first sitting. One of the greatest advantages as a
result of our deals was the birth of a pension scheme for all hourly rated
personnel at Renold – something of which I will always be proud.

Dorothy was now once again suffering with poor health. Complaining
of headaches, she was sent to an ENT specialist and had X-rays by the
score, but no one seemed to find anything wrong and they all therefore
blamed the old scapegoat – 'It's just your age'. Things got worse and worse,
until eventually Dorothy was regularly lapsing into unconsciousness and
she was admitted to hospital. I was called from a management meeting to

be told that Dorothy was going to be moved to Stoke. I raced off to the hospital to be told that it was essential that Dorothy had a brain operation as soon as possible.

The following day, which was a Saturday, I sat in the ambulance with Dorothy and off we went to Stoke. Dorothy asked me, 'What are they going to do to me, duck?' All I could say was, 'They are going to make you better, sweetheart' – how I only hoped they would! We had to stop in a lay-by at Doveridge whilst the ambulance driver attended to Dorothy, but despite the foggy weather we arrived safely. Later that evening, in thick fog, David went over to see his Mum. I went over on the Sunday, and every day for the next sixty-eight days.

Dorothy was in the care of Mr Newton, who would wait to see me and ask all sorts of questions about her – work, home, garden, anything. After a fortnight, on the day before Easter 1972, he said that if all was well on the following day he would operate on Dorothy 'Even I have to be in the right frame of mind and body,' he said. He also told me that as Dorothy had been ill for so long, it was possible she may not survive the operation. Even if she did, I could not be sure she would not lose some of her faculties and could become a complete cabbage.

On my way home, I pulled into a lay-by on the A50. I said a little prayer and decided that I would not tell anyone until the operation was over.

My Mother had passed away and her funeral was taking place the following morning. On that morning, I had a phone call to say that Dorothy's operation had been postponed for twenty-four hours. After my Mother's funeral was over, we were all at the Swan and Jacqueline wanted to come with me to see her Mum. I was trying to deter her, but Aunty Win was egging her on to go, so I asked Kath to take Win on one side and shut her up. I did not want Jacqueline to see her Mum with her head shaved in preparation for the operation. Rod, who was married to my niece Janet (my sister Winifred's daughter), took me to Stoke, driving as if we were in a police chase (he was a police inspector in Derbyshire) and scaring me almost to death.

The next day, I had permission to use a phone in the doctor's room at Renold as often as I wished, and I phoned as instructed at 1pm, 2pm and 3pm, and at last was told that Dorothy was safely back on the ward. I immediately phoned Jacqueline at work and gave her the news, and she said, 'Good old Mum!' I was glad I kept the operation secret until then, because everyone was already worrying enough. I was not allowed to visit that evening, so I spread the good news – as far as it was.

Upon visiting the following day, the sister showed me into a little room to see Dorothy. She was not yet conscious, and what could be seen of her face was black and blue and swollen. I stayed only a minute, then decided to leave her at peace. The sister insisted I go back and talk to Dorothy. She came in with me, took Dorothy's hand and put it into mine, and called out, 'Come on Dorothy, Jim's here!' After a couple of times doing this, there was just a flicker of Dorothy's eyelids. 'That's it!' said the sister, and off she went to fetch Mr Newton. Then I learned that her tumour was so large he had only removed part of it, and if all was well he would operate again in about ten days' time.

On the day of the second operation, I phoned hourly from 2pm until 7pm. At 7.30pm, the hospital phoned me to say that Dorothy was back on the ward and her operation had gone well. When I visited the following evening, Mr Newton was waiting for me and he apologized for keeping me in suspense for so long on the previous day. What on earth can you say to a man who stood for over ten hours doing that type of work to help a complete stranger, and then apologizes?

Whilst Dorothy was gradually recovering and her faculties were returning slowly but surely, life at home was going on – and how!

Keith was sitting his exams as he was nearing school-leaving age. Jacqueline was at work and deputising for Mum on the home front. One of Adrian's school pals had lost his Grandma, and we had a hard time convincing him that his Grandma was OK – as soon as she was able, she phoned him and put his mind at rest.

As for me, I went to Stoke every day, losing time from work, even though I had got to pay for the carpet which we had just had laid in three bedrooms. The economic situation went haywire, inflation became 27½ per cent and my earnings went down. All these things just washed over me because all that mattered was that Dorothy was getting a little better each day; the rest paled into insignificance.

On the plus side, I had much to be thankful for. I had my health, I had my family around me and I found I had many friends I didn't know I had. The people at Renold willed Dorothy back to health; she had so many flowers that the hospital staff asked my permission to disperse them around less fortunate wards. I had lots of people offering to drive me to Stoke to ease things for me and save my expenses.

On 16 May, Alan Patrick, the works personnel officer, came into the factory and said to me, 'A young lady has just phoned me and asked me to make sure that you take her some clothes this evening in order that she can come home with you tomorrow!'

As 17 May was Adrian's birthday, he came with me to fetch Dorothy home – the age of miracles was with us again.

We spent the afternoon and evening very quietly, with only a couple of neighbours visiting us. The first challenge came when it was time for bed. Although Dorothy had been taught to walk again, she had never until now been confronted with climbing a flight of stairs. Not only was it a physical problem for both of us, I was also aware that any fall could be fatal as Dorothy had only half of her skull – the remainder was to be replaced at a later date, the theory being that if it was replaced now as her brain recovered from its months of compression, pressure would build and the pain would return. Obviously I didn't want Dorothy to suspect my fears, in case it should weaken her self-confidence. Off we went up the stairs, with Dorothy pulling on the banister, me behind her also pulling on the banister and helping to lift her with my shoulder under her bottom. Thus the first challenge was overcome; the first of many, the majority of which Dorothy overcame herself with sheer guts and determination.

Dorothy made slow progress. Jacqueline would get her dressed before she went to work, and when her boss learned of the situation he gave her each Monday off in order that she could do the washing etc. As Dorothy improved and became able to dress herself, she would rest a little longer in the morning and would go across to Mrs Copestake at No. 10 to have her dress fastened – and a good old chinwag, I suppose.

It was just prior to Christmas when Dorothy had to go back to Stoke to have the portion of her skull replaced. Mr Newton considered this only a minor operation, and Dorothy was only away for ten days and suffered no setback on her way to fitness.

We had a quiet Christmas, but a happy one, and looked forward to the New Year and hoped for a change and more pleasant times – and we were not disappointed. Dorothy progressed beyond our dreams. I remember she said she would like to have a go at some knitting. Although she had always been able to do this whilst watching TV at the same time, now she didn't know where to start. However, Jacqueline was on hand, and in her own diplomatic and loving way she got through Dorothy's determined attitude of independence and got her going. I asked Jacqueline to buy enough wool for her Mum to knit a jacket which she had seen, because

I knew damn well that Dorothy would not be beaten and would certainly not see the wool go to waste. The tactic worked, and after some tears of frustration and spells of annoyance at her inability, she completed the jacket and was back with her favourite hobby.

In the spring of 1973, Dorothy and I went with a party from Renold to Coventry Theatre, and it was such a thrill to see her laughing and clapping. I was so pleased and so proud that I wrote to Mr Newton and told him of this, and had a hand-written reply.

Keith passed his exams and was due to leave school, and was applying for an apprenticeship as a fitter at several companies. After three or four successful interviews, he chose to come to Renold and was to spend his first year at Technical College.

Dorothy made rapid progress and was discharged by Mr Newton, who was pleased with her desire to return to work on a part-time basis.

So here we were, with all our four children out of school and onto the treadmill of life. We had four grandchildren and were on our way, looking forward to a happy future.

Chapter 9

Better Times

The summer of 1973 was certainly the start of better times for us. Dorothy came back to work at Renold, and was highly embarrassed when Mr Kirkham, a director from Manchester, came onto the shop floor to have a chat to her. He had closely followed her progress during her months away. Keith was settling in at 'Tech'. Jacqueline had a part-time job with Kath and Bert at the Swan. David, with Jean and the two boys, Stephen and Peter, had a house in Lansdowne Terrace (a former home of my father). Roy and Jean, along with Adrian and Karen, were happily settled at Farham Road. All was well with our world.

Jacqueline was 21 in October, and being Jacqueline she did not want a lot of fuss; instead of having a party, she settled for a present of a leather coat from us. As she was still working at the Swan, it was obvious that she would have a few minor celebrations there.

Life having settled into a stable period, everyone appeared to be coping with their individual problems and jogging along comfortably. As for Mum and I, we were managing an annual holiday, enjoying our car trips at weekends and a dance whenever the opportunity arose. By now we were well established and attended all the major functions such as Mayor's Ball, Police Ball, etc. It had become our policy to enjoy life as much as possible, within our means, and to thank God for what we had.

During 1974, Jacqueline had taken a job with Staffordshire Council, which brought her into occasional contact with John, whom she had met at the Swan and who worked at Bass.

It was in June 1974 that I was appointed to the monthly staff at Renold and became foreman of the conveyor assembly section. As I had leap-frogged over many people with longer service, this caused a lot of friction, but as I had not pulled any dirty tricks on anyone I did not let this bother me, apart from the fact that it made life a little uneasy for Dorothy. Eventually the fact became accepted and things settled down, and I enjoyed the challenge and the improvement it made to our living standards.

Romance had blossomed between Jacqueline and John, and when John's Mother passed away in 1975 they decided they would get married. The wedding took place at St John's Church in November 1975, and their first home was a derelict house in Grange Street, which they soon put into a habitable state. So my two walks up the aisle with our daughters was another phase of life completed, and Dorothy and I are grateful and pleased that both are blessed with happiness.

We were also able to purchase No. 7 St Andrew's Drive from the council in 1975, having already bought ourselves a new Ford Consul. After the bleak situation we had been in only a few years ago, we were riding our luck to the limit and determined to make the most of every opportunity – and did so.

Life for Dorothy and I was now very full. All our off-work hours were occupied, with leisure activities taking due priority, and the remainder used for making improvements to No. 7; 1976 was a most enjoyable year for us, and was to be the start of the happiest era of our lives.

In March 1977, Keith became 21 and he and his girlfriend Jackie, who was also 21 in March, decided to have a joint celebration and become engaged. Dorothy and I were quite pleased about this because it meant that we could now envisage all our offspring happily married within our lifetime.

The Silver Jubilee year of Queen Elizabeth II's reign was also in 1977, and huge celebrations took place throughout the year. An ancient method of communication was revived when a chain of huge bonfires were lit along the length of Britain, each one within sight of the next in the chain.

It was the day of these bonfires that Dorothy and I took off from Birmingham airport, along with Jacqueline and John, for a holiday in Austria. This turned out to be the most enjoyable we ever had, and to date (1992) has not been equalled. It was June and we had the benefit of the snow up on the mountains and the spring flowers below. Our hotel at Solden was first class and high up the mountain sides in temperatures of 80°F. We often recall being given a red rose each when we made a purchase in a store. Thinking what a friendly gesture this was, we carefully nursed them for hours all the way home to our hotel, only to be told by the manageress what they stood for. Apparently, a highly volatile political wrangle was taking place over a proposition to build a nuclear power station in the valley to produce electricity. The red rose was the battle symbol of the communist side of the squabble. The power station was never built – or was it ever needed, as Austria already had sufficient power to export to

Germany and others, supplied by hydro-powered generators which cost virtually nothing to operate?

A few weeks after this holiday, a huge air-show in celebration of the Silver Jubilee was held at RAF Finningley. Every squadron in the British Commonwealth was represented, along with Americans, Italians and others who sent their crack display teams. On the day following the private show, the display was repeated for the public, and Dorothy and I went along with Roy, Jean, Adrian and Karen. (It was on this day that Karen stated that she wanted to join the RAF.) An AA official told me that they had received about 5,000 more cars than they had expected – and they coped brilliantly.

Dorothy and Adrian went into an arena to see if they had won a caravan in a raffle, whilst Roy, Jean and Karen went to get the car – and we got separated, hopelessly separated. They left by a different exit and left me behind. Dorothy and Adrian were found by Roy. It ended with me having tannoy announcements, and RAF and civilian police in cars, on motorcycles, etc., all joined in the search. I had a 125mph ride in a police car along the deserted runway, and the police advised me to make my own way home as everyone else had gone and some were returning in full dress for the evening ball. He had less faith in my son-in-law than I had, and at last along came Roy and the rest of our party. The fact that we were last to leave had its compensation in that we were not in the traffic queues.

In 1978 I was made up to superintendent and was responsible for warehousing, transport, despatch and exports. This was brought about because records in warehouse stocks had been in disarray for some years, and the auditors finally had enough and gave the company one last chance to get it sorted or they would close the factory whilst they did it and would prosecute anyone guilty of wrongdoing. Once again, some were surprised I was offered this new post, and many sat back and waited for me to fail to do what all thought was a hopeless task. After a major upheaval, and treading on a few thorns, the next audit not only won acceptance but a recommendation. I was well pleased.

Things moved along in a routine pattern then until 1980. On 6 June it was my 60th birthday. My father had been the first in his family to attain this age, and I was given a nice little party at home by the family.

By now a trading slump was taking place, and in October the company asked for voluntary redundancies from the shop floor. The cash offered to Dorothy was more than she would earn in her last 18 months at work (which included two winters), so she was first to volunteer. Thinking that

Dorothy had special information due to my position, most of the women on her section also volunteered, and I was not popular with their foreman or superintendent.

The downturn in business at Renold meant that four-day working was introduced. This had its advantages because Keith and Jackie were planning to marry and had purchased a house in Tutbury, and I was able to devote my spare time helping to redecorate. One bedroom had a DIY catastrophe in the shape of built-in wardrobes. To dismantle these and rebuild better ones occupied quite a few days, but the pleasure which the result gave to Jackie was just reward.

The year of 1981 was to start an era of change after a long spell of routine lifestyle.

Jackie and Keith were married on 11 July, and perhaps because I had no official duties as when our own daughters were married, I was more aware of the happenings of the day. I recall Jackie walking straight into the midst of a group of handicapped people from the home where she was the cook. I also remember her eating burned toast at her wedding dinner. In the evening celebration at Rolleston School, it was the turn of her Father, Ken, to provide the 'one-off'. After an evening when all had gone well, Ken had been on his best behaviour after getting into the bad books for simply enjoying himself too much at the 21st party! It was midnight when I congratulated him on this after he had just discovered that he had not opened the champagne – and there stood the unopened cases to prove it.

Dorothy and I celebrated our Ruby Wedding on 22 July at the school in Bitham Lane. This brought together long-lost relatives and friends. It was the first big celebration which Dorothy and I had for ourselves, as the war and later financial circumstances had ruled otherwise.

We had over the last few years been able to get away each year for a holiday, and it was as if everything in the garden was lovely. All our family were settled, and we had time to spare and sufficient money to allow us to enjoy life in our new role of 'Darby and Joan'.

Keith and Jackie's son Darryl was born in 1982, and this gave Dorothy the chance to indulge herself as 'Grandma' to the full and spend hours pushing him into the park and around. Being at work had prevented her from doing this with our previous grandchildren, and it took her back to the days when she had done this with our own son, David, for a long time wondering whether or not he would ever see his father – or if he even had a father still alive. Small wonder that she enjoyed the company of Darryl.

Among our circle of friends, Bill Carlrey was to retire from work soon, to be followed by Len Hughes, our friend and neighbour of forty years. I did not have to envy them for long, because I also retired at Christmas 1983. I went into hospital at a minute's notice for a knee operation in October 1983 and was planning to restart work in the New Year, with a view to seeing what the financial situation was with regard to an early retirement.

Dorothy was in town shopping for Christmas when I had a phone call from my manager, who wished to have a chat, so I asked him to come around as I was alone. He made me an offer of early retirement which was above what I was hoping to negotiate, and although I was on the payroll until end of March I did not have to return to work.

We now joined the gang at tea dances at the Town Hall, and with Uncle Lol bowling indoors again at the Town Hall and outdoors at Shobnall. We think these days on the bowling green were some of Lol's happiest times. He particularly enjoyed one afternoon at the Town Hall when, due to meetings taking place, we were using the main hall and a young man came to have a couple of hours' practise on the Wurlitzer. After asking us if we would mind, he carried on. There were only the three of us playing bowls, and Lol really enjoyed the afternoon as he was a keen organ fan and a good pianist himself.

Dorothy and I were now really enjoying life; we had only ourselves to please and no worries at all. The first intrusion into our new-found happiness came in December 1985.

It had been the custom over many years that I went to put up Christmas decorations at the Swan Hotel for my sister Kath and her husband Bert on a Sunday approximately a week prior to Christmas. On this occasion I came home and told Dorothy how ill Bert appeared to be, although he insisted that he was alright. A couple of nights later, we had a phone call around midnight from Kath. Dorothy and I went round to see her to discover that Bert had worked until 11pm and died as he got into bed. He was buried from No. 7 on the day prior to Christmas Eve.

Kath was at this stage not well herself, and I had to take on Bert's role at the Swan. Because of difficulty in getting the tenants out of the house which Kath and Bert were buying for their retirement, this situation lasted until mid-June of 1986. Kath moved into her new home, all newly decorated and carpeted, and her health soon improved considerably. Although I was to become gardener and odd-job man for as long as one could see into the future, it was a great relief from the long hours and strain on both

Dorothy and I of the previous few months. However, we did not now have the complete carefree freedom to which we had become accustomed.

During 1984, Russell had been born to Jackie and Keith in May, and James had arrived for Jacqueline and John in June.

Keith and Jackie, recently having moved to their new home at Norman Road, were always in the throes of making a house into a home. John and Jacqueline were likewise altering and decorating at Abbots Bromley. I could always find work for idle hands. Between the two, Dorothy was always happy as both houses were in pleasant locations, and with jobs at Winshill and the dances on Tuesdays and most Saturdays we had a full life. It was said that appointments had to be made if we were to be found at No. 7!

We were having our annual summer holiday plus a September break at Blackpool, and both Dorothy and I were quite content with our lot and enjoying good health. At times we would take a picnic or just a car ride into our favourite haunts, into the Peaks of Derbyshire, and we would admire the beauty and peaceful serenity, particularly as we could visit in the weekdays. Often we would say, 'To think that all this has been here whilst we have been enclosed in the factory!' We could not be happier than at these times.

Thus we spent the next few years of our lives, and in May 1987 Adrian was 21 and Karen 18, so the family once again had cause for celebration. Dorothy and I had great fun producing cakes in the shape of '21' and '18' and having them decorated, Adrian's to portray his hobbies of dancing and tennis and Karen's her role in the RAF.

By this time Karen was at RAF Cosford, from where I was demobilized. Often we would fetch her on a Friday afternoon for the weekend, and on a couple of occasions I was able to get into the camp and revisit the scenes of my final service days.

During 1987, through the national and local press, all FEPOWs were asked to apply for a medical examination entitled TDI (Tropical Disease Investigation). This was because a disease, strongyloidiasis, which had been known of years ago, was now causing alarm in the aging FEPOW population and a cure had recently been discovered. I applied and was allocated a date in London in January 1988.

On New Year's Eve, 1988 our usual party of dancers were celebrating at the Town Hall. The following morning it transpired that Dorothy's brother, Lawrence, had been admitted to hospital at midnight, having suffered a stroke. As we retired to bed on the night of 1 January, we saw a light flashing through the window, and upon looking out saw Len Hughes being taken to hospital. He had an emergency operation before daybreak – less than twenty-four hours after dancing with us. Thus 1988 did not have a very happy start for us, although both were discharged from hospital about a fortnight later. At around 9pm a few days later, Jenny phoned asking for help as Len was in trouble, so Dorothy and I rushed round. Len was in the bathroom, and he looked up at me and said 'Jim' – the only time in his life in which he called me Jim, as he never lost the habit of 'Mr Banton', which was used when all our children were together. There was nothing I could do but comfort him, and he passed away before the doctor or ambulance arrived. I was unable to attend the funeral as I was due in London for my TDI, and appointments were so valuable they could not be lost (only two per week being granted at each of three hospitals).

On a brighter note, Lawrence was recovering slowly at home when I left for London, and the tests on my examination proved negative. The doctors were more interested in the condition of my knee, and had it photographed and fetched students from another hospital to examine it. (A similar interest was aroused some years later when it was examined at Burton District Hospital.) One evening whilst in London, I had a visit from Karen and her intended Gary, who came all the way from Benson in Oxfordshire where they were now stationed.

I was pleasantly surprised at the improvement in rail travel, as I had not used the railway for many years. Keith and the boys took me to the station and saw me off, and on the journey to London I came into conversation with a Stapenhill man on his way to the Scilly Isles where he was a lighthouse keeper. This intrigued me – a man from the Midlands being a lighthouse keeper – but they had to live somewhere I suppose.

The second fellow at the hospital with me also came from Stapenhill but had travelled by road, and as he was found to have the complaint he had to stay longer.

The year of 1988 turned out to be quite an eventful one. Christopher arrived for John and Jacqueline on 8 March (the anniversary of my date of internment). This arrival appears to be the completion of our family jigsaw, and we now have seven grandsons and one granddaughter.

In November 1988, Karen was married to Gary, who was in the RAF like Karen and in the same trade as her. The first marriage of one of our grandchildren was an occasion, and being attended by a number of Air Force people along with all our family it seemed as if it was designed especially for me – of course it wasn't, although I could not have been more pleased.

Another thing which happened to me in 1988 was that due to going for that TDI in London, I became involved with the Derbyshire PoW Association and also the Java '42 Club, which later led to many happy reunions.

The year of 1989 was one of ups and downs. In early February, my older sister Winifred died after a short illness, and Dorothy's brother Lawrence's health was failing. Lawrence and Sylvia were to celebrate their Ruby Wedding on 9 July but Lawrence was too ill and he passed away on 8 August.

In September, Dorothy and I attended a reunion of FEPOWs at Pontins Sand Bay (near Weston-super-Mare). After a pleasant drive down, we arrived early and took a stroll around. We met a lady with her son and his wife, and as we chatted discovered that her husband had not returned and she knew nothing of his fate. I was later, through the Java Club, able to have her provided with details of his fate. We have become friends for life, and as she lives at Weston Favell close to Dorothy's cousin, we call on her on our visits.

The visit to the Pontins camp will always remain vividly in my mind. We were all strangers bound together with a common bond and the atmosphere was amazing; every man and woman appeared to be as one family – certainly not strangers. The icing on the cake for me was to meet two lads from Sumatra who had been with me right to the end of the line, namely Ray Thompson from Cheadle and Len Williams from Waterlooville.

The reunion with Len was amazing. After making initial contact by a tannoy appeal at breakfast, we met in the lounge along with our wives. As we related to each other the happenings of the day we heard that the war was over, I could see our wives nodding to each other. We both recalled the scenes and used the same words as we had years before to explain to them – it was as if we had rehearsed the same script. Dorothy and Len's wife (also Dorothy) were so pleased to see Len and I reunited, and amazed that we recalled that day exactly as we had each related it to them many years ago. Thinking of it again now, how else could it be told – but honestly?

Dorothy and I also made friends of another PoW from the Derbyshire Association, Herbert Gregory and his wife Elsie, who live at Belper. Herbert had suffered a severe beating whilst in Japan, and is in constant pain today as a result. Coupled with years of continuous pain was the fact that although he had advertised around all the PoW associations, Cilla Black's *Surprise Surprise* on TV, Charlie Chester on the radio, etc., he had failed to find anyone who knew of him or the camp in which he was held. This preyed on his mind, to the extent of causing him to become violent at home at times. I persuaded Herbert to have a notice displayed, and the Pontins manager was very cooperative. As a result, a man who was one of the small party with Herbert presented himself at our table the next day. He later gave Herbert names and addresses of a couple of others. With his mind reassured that it was not all a bad dream, Herbert has now become more settled and rational, and life is better for him and Elsie. We will always be friends of these two couples, and grateful for that week at Pontins. We all gathered at Pontins again in 1990, but people had taken back such good reports from 1989 that several associations came as parties, booked adjoining chalets and tables, and the individual atmosphere was lost completely.

In December 1990, my youngest sister Kath died. She phoned around 11pm for help, and as Dorothy was ill with flu I made for Winshill whilst she contacted Margaret and her husband. As everywhere was locked, the police had to force an entry, but it was already too late. Her funeral took place the day prior to Christmas Eve, exactly as had that of her husband Bert five years before. During 1991 we had the house and its contents to dispose of, which was completed by September.

There were, however, much happier events in 1991. July was the Golden Wedding of Dorothy and I. We were told by our family to present a list of around 100 people with whom we would like to celebrate our great day. Through the following months we learned very little of what was planned, until we were asked to be ready for 6.15pm. Ready we were, and what surprises we had that evening.

At 6.15 prompt, a golden Rolls Royce collected us and took us for a mini tour, whilst those who had seen us off from No. 7 got themselves to the Scout Headquarters at Rolestone to receive us there.

The party of all parties had been arranged. People had come from far and wide: Karen and Gary from Germany, cousins from Wales. There was food and wine in abundance and variety – all prepared by the family themselves. Then came the time for a couple of speeches.

David was given this task, being the oldest, and unfortunately I sat where I could not hear all that was said due to the acoustics, but I did hear him talk of me being a PoW and I had asked that this not be mentioned on the day, so I was none too pleased. However, halfway through his speech he gave me a parcel, and I glanced inside to find a book and a letter from one Colonel Laurens van der Post, with whom I spent some time and whom I greatly admire. When it came to my turn to reply, I was not fully aware of all that David had said, although I had gathered that Dorothy had also had a letter from Mr Newton, who had performed a miracle operation to save her life a few years previously.

Thus I got to my feet, full of pride at the things our family had arranged, full of emotion and only half aware of what had been said. As a result, I'm afraid I rambled on much longer than was polite.

That was the day of all days and a celebration of all celebrations, and when we look back at what care, thought, ingenuity and hard work had gone into it, we always cherish the love with which they all worked to give us such a wonderful day.

One more of my wishes, which was overruled, was an announcement in the *Burton Mail*. Instead, we were given a full-page report and photograph, and to be honest we were pleased about that too.

It is now 1997 and I am surprised that it is so long since I did any work on this part of the project, although I have done some on the second volume.

Life has gone on in the same pattern. We have had a least one holiday per year. A couple of years ago we had a coach holiday, going through France for a one-night stay. Perhaps due to my eternal dislike of all things and people French, our room happened to be a few yards away from a railway station, and from around two o'clock in the morning sleep was an impossibility.

From the ridiculous to the sublime, we journeyed into Switzerland for a few days. Here the hotel was first-class in every aspect: the rooms were huge, with every mod-con, and the scenery absolutely beautiful, as we faced a ski slope at the foot of the mountains. In the distance we could see cable-cars operating at what appeared to me an impossible height. I asked if people used this or if it was for engineering workers, and I was told, 'Tomorrow you will be on it.' When tomorrow came, on it I was. Arriving at the top, we found a large cafe, and looking over the edge, a railway station was so far down that the trains looked like toys. We spent about an hour or so walking and admiring the scenery before we boarded the train to take us down to the other side of the mountain, where our coach had been brought round to collect us. We had a few wonderful days in Switzerland, with boat trips on Lake Lucerne, before we moved into Germany for the last two days of a wonderful tour. At this hotel, a band had been brought in specially to accommodate the English liking of dancing. On the second night we were joined by a party of German holidaymakers, and Dorothy and I ended up teaching a few of them to dance the Square Tango.

Like all good things, the end arrived all too soon and the following day we started for home. Over the years we have had some wonderful holidays, but this one seemed to surpass them all. Unfortunately, we now had to start the long journey home, and as we had to cross the whole length of France, get on the ferry and be home in one day, it was very tiring. We arrived home at 3am, and I was due at the clinic to have a toe nail removed at 9am —a case of from the sublime to the ridiculous!

Later, we had a long weekend in London and included a visit to the theatre.

I said at the start of this work that it would not be in chronological order, and after such a long time since I last worked on this manuscript you will see by the following pages just what I mean. However, I have made up my mind to devote the winter weather to catch up.

Whilst I am on the subject of holidays, I will tell of those which hold fond memories for both Dorothy and me. I have mentioned the meeting up with a pal from Sumatra days by the name of Len Williams, an ex-naval man. In 1993, we decided to have a holiday down with Len and his wife, so we booked ourselves into a place called The Smugglers Haunt on Hayling Island in Hampshire. On the Thursday of the week, we were invited to attend a meeting of Hayling Island FEPOWs, which is held monthly at the British Legion Club in their very well-equipped premises. As a guest, I was obliged to stand up and say who I was and where I lived, and give a short account of my whereabouts as a FEPOW. As I stood to do this, I rested my hand on the edge of the table, which made it tremble a bit. Upon seeing this, Len's wife Dot said to Dorothy, 'He should get a pension for that, you know', and it was on her insistence that I did. After the meeting, we retired to the dining-room and had a very good three-course lunch. Later in the week, we took Graham (the son of Dorothy's cousin Shelagh) and his wife Jenny to meet Len at Waterlooville, as they were both in the Navy, although Jenny had left upon getting married.

This evening turned out to be one of those occasions which one will always remember and think back on. The party, without any pre-arranging, found itself split into two: ladies at one end of the room and men at the other. Dot entertained the ladies, relating how she and Len had been involved with all the stars who had made the film *The Yangtze Incident*, and had met them and all the Royals at the movie's premiere. This had come about because Len had been the official naval adviser when it was being made.

Before I leave this part of the story, I must tell you of an incident which happened on the night of the premiere and was reported in the press. As Len lined up with all those to be presented to the Queen and Prince Philip, after the Queen had passed, Philip asked him what ship he was on at present. 'The Royal Yacht, sir,' Len answered. 'I have dropped a right b******!' said Philip. He had been briefed on Len before he started, and as it was all being recorded the Queen and the rest of the party all had to go back and start again – 'The Ladyship [the Queen] was not amused!' Len told me.

Back to the British Legion Club, at the other end of the room, Len was telling Graham the story of the action of the Chinese capture of HMS *Amethyst* by the Chinese, and how he and the skipper planned and made their escape. The newspaper headlines read 'Kerns on the bridge and Len on the engines'. Graham was asking how they managed to black out the ship whilst they prepared their getaway. Len said that after they had got to a more hospitable area, they were able to get some vital oil supplies. The difficulty was that it was in barrels, and Graham was interested to learn how Len got it into his tanks. Whilst all this was going on, I was sat between the two groups, fascinated by both conversations. Len's son was keeping us all supplied with drinks, alcoholic and otherwise. It seemed like only a few minutes had passed when I looked at my watch and informed the company that it was now almost 2am. I will always be glad that I arranged that get-together, because it was of interest to the ladies as well as the men.

In 1995 it was the 50th anniversary of the end of the war, and we had the celebrations of both VE Day and VJ Day. The first celebration we had was a day at RAF Cosford. This was particularly pleasing to me, because not only was it the station from which I was demobbed but it was also where my only granddaughter Karen did her trade training when joining the RAF. This day of reunion came about by the efforts of the wife of an ex-FEPOW who does a vast amount of work on our behalf. The lady is Pam Stubbs, who has taken it on herself, and succeeded, to trace every RAF FEPOW who came home, finding out how and where they were released and how they got home. Neither the RAF nor the War Office had records of this, and she worked on it for years. On this occasion, Pam got in touch with the Air Minister and asked if he would do something by way of a celebration for us. As it was fairly central, and because all returning RAF personnel had come through there, it was decided Cosford was an ideal location. Some sixty FEPOWs and our wives spent the day around the camp and the museum, and had a traditional service meal of sausage and mash, with the added perks of starters and afters, plus as much drink as you thought it was safe for you to cope with. A group of German PoWs from a society in London also joined us. By coincidence, Karen's husband Gary was at Cosford on a course, and he spent his lunchtime serving drinks with us. After the lunch, a flying display was laid on for us, with a few aerobatics and an exhibition of wing walking. I was pleased to see the only remaining Bristol Blenheim on the scene, and was taken back to 1940–41 when its engines spluttered into life as it warmed up to have a mock battle with an ME 109.

By collecting information from FEPOWs, Pam has been able to trace most of the movements of the PoWs during captivity and intends to publish it. When this happens, I will of course buy a copy. The project is on hold at present as Pam is recovering from a hip-replacement operation.

Also at Cosford was Jim Kirkwood, who was with me at Kluang in Malaya, and although we were not aware of it at the time, was also with me at Kalidjati. As we stood around talking on the airfield, I heard a man behind me talking of Kalidjati, and when his conversation finished I asked him how and when he had got away. He said that he found a petrol bowser, so I asked if he remembered giving a chap a lift; he did, so I shook his hand and thanked him after fifty years.

Then of course came VE Day, which passed Burton with little more than a service at the Memorial Grounds by the Royal British Legion. For VJ Day, Len and his wife invited us down to their service on Hayling Island, so we booked in at The Smugglers Haunt again. Once again, Dorothy and I had a wonderful time with them.

For the meeting at the British Legion Club, Dorothy and I decided to take a taxi as Len had the job of escorting a lady from the War Pensions Authority who had asked if she would be welcome. We had a most wonderful service which was conducted by the local vicar. The usual remembrances were made, and we came to the Two-Minutes' Silence. As this ended, a lone piper in the distance began to play 'Flowers of the Forest', and as the volume reached a crescendo the band struck up with the hymn 'Oh God our Help in Ages Past'. As we sang the hymn, the Union Jack and the standard of the Royal British Legion were raised from their salute. This was one of those moments when I swallowed heavily and reached for my handkerchief. Dorothy whispered, 'Are you alright, duck?', as she always does on these occasions.

At the conclusion of the service, those of us who were mobile walked across the road to lay wreaths on a little war memorial round the corner. As we walked back and came to cross the road, the traffic in either direction stopped to let us cross. Once again, I had to swallow hard because this was a spontaneous gesture in respect of the badges and medals we were wearing.

Next it was back to the dining-room for a banquet. After the meal, a few short speeches were made and another touching episode took place. A young lady was called to the table to be presented with some medals. It had become known that her father had never claimed his medals, and without her knowledge these had been acquired for her by the FEPOW Association. Now it was her turn to swallow and take deep breaths.

As soon as the proceedings were over, Len said that if we looked sharp we would be able to get to Portsmouth before they began their celebrations. Having been around that area all his life, he knew how to get around all the bottlenecks. We arrived in the midst of what seemed to me to be a hopeless situation. However, the gods and the police were on our side when a policeman stepped in front of us and even apologized for doing so, again I suppose because we were wearing our blazers, etc. The reason he had stopped us was that the parade was coming. It passed right in front of our car, giving us a grandstand view. That having passed, we drove on, hoping to find a parking space. Once again the gods smiled on us; we had not gone far when someone was trying to get out, and Len courteously obliged and we took his place. We were right in front of the ferry terminal, and Len was all for us going over to the Isle of Wight. I said, 'I'm not getting on board any ship with you – you get the damned things sunk!' We sat there and watched the release of thousands of red, white and blue balloons, for which people had paid a pound each. The money raised was to go to various charities for ex-service associations. We had some up there, but even Dorothy with her inspector's eyes could not see them. Len then took us on a tour of the sights and scenery around Portsmouth and home for tea. It was when we arrived there that I think I heard the ladies talk for the first time all afternoon. We were assured that they had enjoyed every minute of the day, and I am sure that they had. Once again they had supported their men-folk in the way for which over many years they have won the esteem of FEPOWs nationwide.

During the rest of the week, Len and Dot took us around each day. On one occasion we went to Chichester, and after a look around the cathedral we went into the cafe for the proverbial cup of tea. Here one of those little incidents of life which always stick in your mind happened. All the food was presented each day by various firms around the city, and all the labour was voluntary. Ice cream was 30p per portion, which consisted of two scoops, and there was a choice of vanilla or strawberry. The ladies of course wanted a portion of mixed. This threw the waitress into utter confusion, and she dashed off to seek advice from the chief. After some discussion, it was decided that a portion could consist of one of each flavour at no extra charge. Another day we went through some most beautiful scenery to an 'olde worlde' restaurant miles away from anywhere. We sat in the window, looking out across a lovely valley. Len said that they often went there for a meal simply because of the scenery. A helicopter came in and landed on a nearby field, and two men got out to have a meal in their lunch hour. That's how the other half live.

Once again it was time for all good things to come to an end, and we had to say our goodbyes. This had been another special week's holiday. I had met many friends; some new ones and some longer-standing ones. Everyone had their own quiet moments, kept their thoughts to themselves, no one looked for sympathy or glory and we all knew that each and every one of us was thinking the same thing – 'Will we see each other again, and if so, when?'

The next day, it was time to say our goodbyes to Dot and Len. They had given us another wonderful welcome. As Len had given up driving long distances, we knew that he would not be coming to Burton, and I was also getting older and doubting my courage to tackle the trip again. Our two ladies had been wonderful, as always, and they must have had the same thoughts. As Len and I shook hands and hugged each other, it was obvious that we both wondered if it was our final farewells. After we had shared so much, there exists a bond which only those who have experienced it can appreciate. We had not had a brief encounter; we had lived together, worked together and helped each other when either of us was in extra trouble. The Bible says, 'Greater love hath no man than this, that a man lay down his life for his friends', and this we all did.

Since getting involved with the FEPOW organizations, I have come across many old friends and made many new ones. Herbert Gregory from Belper, whom I met in Derby, is suffering more and more from the injury to his spine as a result of a beating by a Japanese guard. Jim Kirkwood, who I was with at Kluang and Kalidjati, passed away a few months ago, and each time we get a newsletter we read of more who have left the fold. It is a question of the great big saw getting nearer and nearer. On the other side of the coin, I have been reunited with more of the old brigade. About a year ago, Keith made a contact for me with Andy Berry, whom I was with at Massingham and went out to Singapore with. Later he put me in touch with a chap who had been the navigator of the Sunderland on which I flew to Ceylon after leaving Sumatra. As I sat reading on a Sunday afternoon a few weeks ago, I had a phone call from a chap by the name of Dougie Denham, who had been in the same billet as me at Kluang. He too is in a poor way, as a result of having a stroke. He had seen an article which I had written for the *Java News*. We sat and recalled all the names of the people who had shared the hut with us, and so it goes on.

The icing was put on the cake when we returned from the week at Portsmouth. Karen's husband, Gary, had got in touch with one of my long-lost cousins living in Oxford, of whom I had not seen or heard for about thirty years. As a result, Dorothy and I went to visit them. He had got his two brothers and their wives to join him, and we had a good hour or two together. Sadly, Norman's wife passed away on Boxing Day last year.

The finding by Keith of Andy Berry and the navigator are worthy of an explanation. At the time, Keith was working at Lloyds Bank in High Street, and he called in on us as he was on his way to work at about 8.45 one morning. He asked if I knew where Andy lived, but all I could tell him was that the last I knew he was living in Carlisle. I was in the kitchen washing the breakfast dishes about half an hour later, when Dorothy called me to the phone as Andy wanted to speak to me. Keith had got in touch by ringing the office of the Carlisle Registry, they gave him an address to try and he was successful. Keith told me that when he asked Andy if he remembered me, Andy said, 'Yes – No. 956528, of course I know him.' When Keith said he was surprised that he had remembered my number correctly, Andy said that it was because I was the only one with six figures, whilst everyone else had seven. Of course we have kept in touch, and I learned that Andy had lost two wives, and that he had worked for many years as a male nurse. A few weeks ago, I had a call from Andy after I had failed several times to get through to him. He said, 'I was at the local races cheering the horses, and awoke to find myself in the Intensive Care Unit of the local hospital. The sickening part of it was that the blessed horse had lost my money.' It was obvious that Andy was just the same as he always had been. Thankfully, he has now got over his illness.

The story of the navigator is even more amazing. Keith was paying his first call on a new customer, and in the chat before business was started was asked what he thought about working for a Japanese company. 'Why?' asked Keith. The chap said that his father simply could not stand them, and he proceeded to say that his father was flying on Sunderlands during the war and had picked up a load of PoWs who had worked on the Sumatra Railway. They had to take them from Singapore to Colombo, and he was disgusted at the condition of them. As this was a one-off flight, it was obvious that I was one of them and therefore the contact was made.

Even after all these years, such things keep cropping up and it is only right that they should be recorded. There is another story of how we were discovered in Sumatra, which I will tell in the last chapter.

P.S. Because these stories continue to turn up even after fifty years, this story is told elsewhere in more detail than I could hope to do myself. I noticed the reissue of a book first published some years ago entitled *Prelude to the Monsoon*, which was written by one of the men who came into the camp, and which I strongly recommend you read.

Chapter 10

The Price of Progress

Having passed my three score years and ten, and with time on my hands, I often sit and recall the events and changes which have taken place in my lifetime. I am certain that all such changes, clever as they may be reputed to have been, have not been so advantageous to life as we are given to believe. All the so-called advantages have extracted a price for which future generations will have to pay. As I describe each one, I hope you will understand what I mean, even if you may not altogether agree with me.

The things which come most readily to mind are: motor cars, jet engines, electricity power stations, war, the reorganization of schools, medicines, and the National Health Service. I suppose that already you are surprised that of the thousands of alternatives, these should be first mentioned. I will try to explain how they have impressed me and the strange experiences which have influenced my thinking. I will try to do things in some kind of order, but as I intend to add to this until it is time to 'take my boots', I cannot guarantee this.

The first major change in my life came with the reorganizing of schools. I started at Victoria Road Infants, and was due to progress via Victoria Road Boys until I left for work at 14 years of age – unless I was lucky enough to be selected to go to a secondary school in Guild Street or Broadway, or if my parents could afford it I may go to the Boys' Grammar School in Bond Street.

The monument to that era lies in the headstones over the doorways. In York Street, one says 'Infants' and another says 'Girls', while a third in Victoria Road says 'Boys'. Each one had its own separate playground.

With the introduction of the new system, which meant entrance to secondary and grammar schools would be via an examination known as the 'Eleven Plus', I was transferred to Grange Street because I was 9 years old.

Those who passed the Eleven Plus would go to Guild Street or Broadway Central, or some boys to the Grammar School, with girls going to the High

School in Waterloo Street, both of the latter of which are still there today. Of those who did not make the grade or refused the chance, boys would go to Victoria Road and girls to Goodman Street. Boys and girls were not allowed to walk to school together.

I progressed to Guild Street, which was reckoned much the better of the two secondary schools. This meant that I would have to stay until I was 15. At this time, an extra year at school was no small sacrifice by parents. The extra 14 shillings a week which a 14-year-old would earn would make a vast difference to the living standards of the whole family. I have always been grateful to my parents for giving me the opportunity. The advantages of going to Guild Street were immense. We were taught subjects beyond the three 'Rs' such as physics, chemistry, French, shorthand, typewriting and bookkeeping. Our physics and chemistry laboratories were in the tall library building which stood in Union Street, which is now a car park opposite Sainsbury's. We also had the art studio and woodwork rooms in a building behind there.

I was pleased to go to my new school, although the work was more difficult and much had to be done as homework. Discipline was strict. We wore uniforms of a green cap with a coloured 'house button' on top and a green blazer with a GCSE badge on the pocket in silver.

Anyone who misbehaved or brought the school into any disrepute soon suffered the wrath of headmaster Mr C.E. Binns (known as 'Chassar'). Punishment was additional homework or six of the best – or both.

In those days, only the Grammar School had its own playing field, and we used the Ox-Hay.

Our maths and shorthand teacher was a lay preacher by the name of A.P. Bakewell. He took his retribution by having you either rewrite huge passages from your exercise book or get a thick-ear. Weighing some 18 stone, he had hands like a side of beef. If you ducked, he would stand on your foot whilst he had another go. Needless to say, he had few errant pupils at his lectures.

'Doffy', as he was known, also taught typing, for which we had to take 45-minute classes before normal school hours as it was optional. During our last year, he had an operation for a cancer in his mouth. As by now we were achieving reasonable shorthand speeds, this made life difficult for him and for us. It was obvious that he realized this, as he became much more tolerant. He was a good master, as were all of them.

The French master was a Mr Sauvain, who lived in the round bungalow on Rolleston Road. He was very good to a lad from 'The Boy's Home', an orphanage on Belvedere Road. He used to invite him to do some gardening work at weekends, always telling him to come to the back door.

The chemistry master was Jackie Cannel, who lived on Newton Road and spent his lunchtime in the Swan Hotel. Afternoon sessions with him were always fun, to say the least. During the war, he was caught with a 'still' in the laboratory. He collapsed on the bus on his way to school and died.

W.E. Ridgeway (art) and C.J. Lawley (English) doubled as sports organizers, whilst Clem Whiles and I alternated as captain and vice-captain for Rodney House.

Then came the war, and at one time one of the many successful pupils from this school, Air Commodore Staton, was my AOC; on one occasion I had the pleasure of being his chauffeur, and he was pleased when I told him that I had been a 'Golliwog' like him. He also gave me the money for a good night out.

So I arrived home, the war in Europe and the celebrations had finished six months ago, and the foreign troops had almost all gone home. It was a strange kind of normality which was returning, and I was soon aware that things would never be as they were before September 1939.

You must realize that for four years I had been out of our regular world – no news of the progress of the war or the changes of the lifestyle of people, and no experience of the changes of people or anything at all in life. One by one I heard of people who would not come back and of things that no longer were.

It seemed that children no longer played happily in the street, as I had done in my time. On the Outwoods Recreation Ground or at Stapenhill, the bands no longer played for dancing on Saturday evenings or for people to sit and listen on Sundays.

I was bewildered, and I must admit I was somewhat scared. It was only the love and patience of Dorothy and our two families which kept me going through the next year or so. I would sit for hours mentally trying to sort out what was wrong. Eventually I realized that during a period of about five or six years, people had accepted changes and adapted to them gradually. I had long and often dreamed of home as I had left it, but now I had to learn overnight all the changes and how to live with them. This was a shock with which many FEPOWs could not cope. Thanks to Dorothy, I was taught to realize that it was all in the past, and that I had got to learn to live in the new world. I hope that in the ensuing years I have returned her love and rewarded her patience.

What had also changed was the attitude of people and their acceptance of a regimented lifestyle. They were content with the fact that life was improving because some food and goods were becoming available in the shops.

So far they had not realized that the technology developed as a necessity of war was about to be released into civil use. There were huge factories standing idle waiting to be retooled to produce goods for domestic consumption, not only in England but also in America.

Work was plentiful, and everyone was anxious to earn as much as possible in order to purchase the goods as fast as they became available – furniture, clothes and eventually cars. Now we have the birth of what was to be the scourge of the world for at least the remainder of the century – inflation, brought about by demand being greater than supply. From this, the wheel goes full circle and overproduction brings unemployment. Thus we will return to the same situation we had in the 1930s.

In the last fifty years of the twentieth century, the world was seen to advance more than it had in the previous nineteen-and-a-half centuries.

Although the war was over, the world was not at peace. There was great mistrust of the Russians by Britain and America (and vice versa). The liberated countries of Europe and Germany were wary of each other. China was making noises in the Far East. We were also witnessing the end of colonialism, with each country demanding its freedom from it. Thus we began to see the ending of the empires of Britain, France and Holland, which was not to be achieved without bloodshed.

I had volunteered to join the RAF early in the war (having already joined the RAFVR), and I am not going to relate more of my experiences than is necessary to point out how they influenced the rest of my life and my reasoning.

The most noticeable effect it had had on me is that I am not the light-hearted, happy-go-lucky person who had enjoyed his teens. I had become very sombre and deep-thinking. But I had all my limbs and was amongst the lucky ones of my era.

It is impossible to describe to those who have not experienced 'service life' what is meant by the RAF motto '*Per ardua ad astra*' ('Through adversity to the stars') and its esprit de corps; even more emphasis was put on this by the war.

During the summer of 1940, I was on one of the many new airfields at Massingham in Norfolk. The weather was fantastic, the two squadrons – No. 18 and No. 101 – were busy and everyone got stuck in to do whatever wanted doing. We became an instant happy family made up of a bunch of strangers, all with a common cause. I drove petrol bowsers and bomb trolleys when not on duty in my own job of 'Fire and Rescue'. Whatever job that needed doing was done by the nearest pair of hands without needing to be asked or told.

Then came one evening in September during the Battle of Britain. We were watching the Blenheims[1] take off into the beautiful summer sunset when tragedy struck. A couple of German raiders caught us unawares. We had received no warning, and suddenly these planes were amongst ours, which were taxiing and taking off. Bombs and machine guns were making the noises of war. All we could do was fall flat on our faces and hope. After perhaps ten or fifteen minutes, it ceased and the noise changed to that of engines running and people shouting. Then it changed again; the engines had gone quiet and it was the noise of people shouting and running to the aid of those in trouble. In a short time, the injured were taken away or being treated on the spot. A couple of lads had been killed, one of whom had been working with me. Although I had experienced air raids before, this was my baptism of gunfire; I realized how fickle life was, how soon it could end, and that no one was immune from war.

I remember afterwards that I was not frightened, and I wondered why. I eventually decided that it was the camaraderie that was shown, and that people could, under stress, count on each other. The effects that this and other such instances had on my life are two-fold. I am content with what I have, and I find it difficult to tolerate people who bemoan their hard luck and are not prepared to try to alter it. There are always a million people worse off.

Then came along another lasting impression, of an entirely different kind but one just as important.

In the summer of 1941 I went to Malaya, and this certainly caused a lasting change to my outlook on life, but again, may I emphasize, not due to the war side of life there.

Malaya was beautiful and the Malays intriguing. They had a saying which summed up their attitude to life and the way they lived it far better than hours of explanation ever could. It was '*Tida Appa*'. Strictly translated, it

---

[1] The Bristol *Blenheim* was a British light bomber aircraft.

means 'It doesn't matter'. The troops adopted this saying, and everyone became '*Tida Apperish!*'

The Malays were so laid-back it was unbelievable. You could follow any path off any road and come across a *Kampong* (hutted village), and you would be made welcome. Soon, we were all able to cope with their language as it was so descriptive (i.e. a train was *kereta api*, a 'wagon of fire').

They were content to just grow sufficient food to keep themselves. They did not wish to interfere with the rest of the world, not did they wish the rest of the world to interfere with them. They just thought, '*Tida Apa*'.

Unfortunately, the world was about to interfere with them. It would change their way of life, but it would take generations to change their attitude to it.

The Malays would not hurry; they did not walk as Westerners did, they just ambled along at their own pace. They had little, asked for no more and were blissfully happy with the peace and beauty of their homeland. Alas, they were soon to become 'piggy in the middle' of a war between two countries of which they knew nothing, and cared less.

After being ravaged by conflict, this country has gained vastly from the advances made by war. They quietly became as prosperous as any people in the world. Has it changed the Malays? Not a bit of it – they just say '*Tida Appa*'.

Earth roads have now been replaced by six-lane motorways, and they have all the trappings of modern science and technology. The Malays think all that is for tourists, and after a day's work in the new factories and hotels, they amble back to their homes, which now have TV sets and electricity, etc.

I have tried to point out how the same technology which through greed has brought unemployment to the Western world has brought prosperity and peace to Malayans. But how long will it last? They will soon be the victims of overproduction, and the natives will return to poverty. Having tasted the good things in life, they may not take kindly to losing them, and may not be prepared to say '*Tida Appa*'.

It must not be forgotten that after the war, Malaya was in turmoil for a long time because of its riches. It produced vast amounts of tin and rubber. Britain was reluctant to lose this, and the Malays, like many other countries, demanded their independence. Due to the nature of its terrain, a long and bitter jungle war was fought, only for the obvious inevitable outcome to emerge.

All these things, whether I like it or not, have helped make me what I am today.

The Internal Combustion Engine

The internal combustion engine and its rapid development brought about the motorcar and in turn the lorry and the omnibus. What an impact they have had on the world and our individual lives.

Before I went to school, I had an operation at the General Infirmary. I was taken in by an ex-army ambulance with canvas sides, and later fetched home in a bullnose Morris by Miss Bull, the daughter of the landlord of the Napier pub at 14 Victoria Street. Few other kids could lay claim to such fame as either of these rides. This would be about 1924.

The arrival of the bus of course brought about the end of the trams. I remember coming out of Victoria Road School and seeing my first bus. It was a No. 5 bound for Branstone Road via Waterloo Street and Station Street. It was just an oblong box on wheels, but the bus service brought transport to such places as Derby Street and Shobnall Street as it required no tracks. Furthermore, it could cope more ably with the snow, which always plagued the tram service.

It was obvious that as progress was made with the motorcar, people would soon wish to prove which one was best and who was the best driver. The earliest racetrack which I can remember was an oval circuit at Brooklands. The monotony of just going round and round soon led to road racing, and one of the finest tracks in the world was built at Donington. As a youth, I spent many happy days there and the rapid increase of speed was astonishing. I saw the finest drivers and cars in the world right up to 1939.

By the time the war came along, many people were using cars and lorries to replace horses. The horse had a reprieve when petrol became scarce, but it was to disappear when petrol came off ration when the war was over.

Cars and lorries, like many other things, were developed rapidly as a necessity of war. Thousands of ex-service vehicles were sold off cheaply when hostilities ceased, and many new transport companies came into being as a result. One particular vehicle that owes much of its development to war needs was the tractor, which with adaptations has since taken over not only from horses but also other machines on farms.

The demise of the horse meant the loss of jobs and skills for farriers and wheelwrights, coach builders, harness makers and stable lads etc.

Then as lorries got larger and, like cars, more numerous, new roads had to be built. The next obvious progression was the loss of rail traffic to a faster and door-to-door road transport. So as railway wharfs closed, road transport depots opened up. It is of great satisfaction to me that new jobs were made to make up for those lost by the railways.

Before we leave the internal combustion engine, let us not forget the importance of its development and the part it played in our war effort.

As the jet engine was not as yet sufficiently developed, petrol and the diesel versions were our only forms of power. They powered all our aircraft, ships, tanks and each new vehicle for whatever purpose they were invented. With the end of the war, all this technology became available to the motor industry. Not only did it vastly improve the cars, it also speeded the production. Road vehicles were fitted with such luxuries as heaters, direction-indicators and —the biggest boon to drivers – synchromesh gears, so driving was made much more easy and less tiresome.

Later came the age of the microchip and the computer, so the road vehicle became a very different animal. To accommodate the vastly increasing numbers of vehicles and their speeds, miles of new and better roads had to be built. With all of this, of course, had to come a whole host of new legislation and speed restrictions, and a larger and more modern police force to enforce them – or at least try to.

So, what is the price we have to pay for these advances? First of all, we find that all our countryside is scarred with miles and miles of concrete and asphalt roads. Then in our towns and cities we have the atmosphere polluted with toxic fumes. Then we have traffic either brought to a standstill or crawling along, being overtaken by those who still use their legs for what they are intended and walk. After that we find that the only solution is to 'let the train take the strain'. A good many influential people are already advocating this.

The difference which this made to my childhood and that of my children is as follows.

We used to play in our streets, rarely disturbed by cars, none of which were ever parked in the streets. The boys would play football, or cricket against a lamp post. The girls would skip, sometimes the rope tied to a drainpipe, lowering the rope to let people pass. Another difference is that people would say 'thank you' with a smile; alas today they would not be so accommodating. Other times there would be mixed teams of boys and girls playing rounders, and often mothers would stand talking to neighbours as they watched (and were sometimes called upon to adjudicate a tight decision). Boys would find a hole between the bricks of the pavement and play marbles; a box of twenty-five would cost a penny. Turns would be taken to roll a marble at the hole, and whoever was the nearest would be first to attempt to roll the remainder in by using a bent forefinger. The player who rolled in the last marble was declared the winner and would collect all those from the hole.

As we got older, we would be allowed to go to the Outwoods Recreation Ground to play. There was a train from Bass Shobnall which left at eight o'clock, and that was my designated time to leave for home. It was always to blame for me being late home. Little did I realize that a few years later I would play a part in getting that train together when I became an engine driver at Bass Worthington.

In the winter months, a 'play centre' was held at the school, where we could play games, paint, draw etc. in the safety and warmth.

One other thing which disappeared with the horses, of course, was the deposit which they left on the roads! The more enterprising and less discerning lads would collect this, and get tuppence per bucket selling it as manure. The more ambitious ones would earn a shilling for taking a barrow-full to an allotment. A shilling was equal to 5p in today's currency.

Before the war, there used to be so many kids playing on the Outwoods Rec that it was often difficult to find a space. Now I go over and don't see a soul playing unless it is organized, with goal posts provided for a nominal fee.

When I walked over there a few weeks ago, the only people I saw were half a dozen kids about 10 years old. They were setting fire to the dry grass on the canal side and waiting for the fire brigade to arrive. I am glad that I was born in more well-behaved times, because we had much more fun.

Dorothy and I are eternally grateful that our children and grand-children – and we are sure our great-grandchildren – will all know how to enjoy life in a civilized and well-behaved manner.

The Jet Engine

Because this engine is so widely used to power our present-day aircraft, we tend to forget all the other advantages it has brought that we now take for granted. Before we go into that, we should not forget that it was a British invention, the brainchild of one Frank Whittle. His work was not recognized until late in his life, when he was granted a knighthood, having spent most of his life in America.

The idea came to him when he was using a blowlamp in his workshop. This was a device whereby a gas was produced by heating paraffin under pressure, and was used for soldering and burning off paint etc. I am almost certain that the first jet engine was flown from a field in Church Broughton, where I recall photographs of it hanging in a public house. It was definitely built by Rolls-Royce at Derby, who are still the leaders in this field.

Something that is certain about jet-powered aircraft is that when we were 'guests' of the Emperor of Japan in Java, a few lads who had come out after us were adamant that they had seen planes flying without propellers. Although everyone scoffed and poured scorn on them, they would not be moved from their story. Eventually, it was felt that they had too much sun on the way over! Yet time has proved that they were right all along. I wonder how often those lads have told the story of how they were not believed, that is if any of that small group came home safely.

It would be impossible for me to list all the advantages of the jet engine that we today take for granted, and I don't intend to try. You can while away many idle moments trying to think what is and what is not a by-product of that invention. Let me start you off. It was developed to power the rockets which enabled us to put a man on the moon. Then you think of all the spin-offs from that. I can dial my pal in Canada and he answers in seconds and I can sit in my chair and watch events taking place on the other side of the world, all by the use of satellites launched by jet propulsion.

So many things which are now used in everyday life have derived from the invention of Sir Frank Whittle.

Alongside the developing of the jet engine in order to get to the moon, scores of other things came as by-products, such as Teflon, which gives us non-stick frying pans and saucepans.

As I have said, it is impossible to count all the related benefits which we enjoy, but before I leave them I would like to return to the telephone. Before satellites, miles and miles of cables had to be laid under oceans and land, at terrific cost and effort. Owing to the rapid increase of the use of the telephone, these cables were so congested that they were inadequate before they were completed. The system was so congested that one had to wait hours trying to get a line. It was so bad that business people would book a call at additional cost in order to get in the queue.

For the 'price of progress', I think the jet engine was easily the best value invention the world has seen. We have sacrificed only a few acres of land, and as the noise and pollution levels of jet engines are constantly being reduced, so too is the 'price' reduced. Furthermore, every human being receives a benefit, in the home, in hospital treatment etc. It reaches every aspect of our lives and we don't even notice the cost.

The Power Industries

The producers of power – gas and electricity – were both housed in adjacent plants in Wetmore Road alongside the River Trent, and were serviced by a communal railway line. They both operated at a profit, and as they were owned by the local council they contributed to its budget. This source of revenue was lost when they became nationalized.

I must deal with them separately, starting with gas. Anything to do with gas was dealt with by local workmen, from production to installation, and of course the collection of the cash from the meters in each house. These meters were operated by inserting a penny coin into the slot – that was one old penny by the way. In my early days of life, every house cooked and was lit by gas. The light was produced by means of a mantel. This was a cup-shaped object made of a gauze impregnated with some form of chemical which made it very brittle and thus difficult to handle. Many was the tragedy of a broken mantel. It usually fell to be my lot to fetch a new one from the corner shop, and the hazard was not helped by the taunting of other kids – but they would have their turn. Despite the frailty of these things, they were extremely efficient, so much so that years later Dorothy's uncle, a tailor, refused an alternative during the conversion to natural gas. To produce the gas, truckloads of coal would be emptied into hoppers on their way into the ovens, where it was cooked to extract the gas. The gas was then stored in huge cylindrical holders until used. The extraction of the gas from the coal left a clinker-like substance known as coke, which was then sold to blacksmiths etc. for their furnaces. Night watchmen who stood guard over road works and so on would have a huge cresset made from discarded coopers' hoops filled with the red glowing coke. In the cold winter nights, passers-by would stop to warm their hands and chat for a few minutes with the custodian. One whom these chaps could always rely on for a few minutes' companionship was the patrolling policeman, especially if the tea was mashed.

When the gas was nationalized, we soon started to see the changes. First of all, the loss of revenue to the council had to be made good, which of course meant an increase on everyone's rates bill. Then came the meddling from people distant from the locality, 'the hidden faces of officialdom'. Soon, to show their authority, it was decided to close Burton's gas production, and our gas was to be supplied from Derby. This meant that everyone at Burton lost their jobs. This procedure became the practice in every other industry.

With the discovery of natural gas under the North Sea, Burton was to become the guinea pig as we became the first town to be converted. New mains had to laid under all the streets. Some household appliances were able to be converted to accept it, but others were too old and had to be replaced with new.

When the plant in Wetmore Road was finally dismantled, the huge mountain of coke which stood in the yard was loaded into railway wagons and was sold to Sweden, which was proof of the value of the by-product.

Where we once had the facilities for buying cookers, gas fires and lighting equipment from our own showrooms, we now have to get them from people who offer no after-sales service. Furthermore, the Gas Board has so reduced its forces in the clamour for profit they cannot supply the service. The situation now is that we have to call on the service of previous workers who have set up their own businesses to do the work.

The Electricity Industry

The nationalization of the electricity industry was absolutely necessary for two very good reasons. Firstly, because the demand for it had increased so much, and would continue to do so as modern methods of production came into use. Secondly, because it was so run-down and out of date that it was unable to meet what was already demanded of it. Factories and homes were constantly being cut off without notice for long periods. The amount of money required to make the present plants capable of supplying what was needed could not possibly be found by the industry itself.

So it was that the government took over the vast building of modern plants. Not only did the new type of power stations full of up-to-date technology soon spring up all over the country, but a massive complex of pylons and cables were also needed to distribute the output to the homes and industry. Though it was to be commended for the speed at which the task was undertaken, we were later to count the cost – in more ways than one.

Firstly, due to the large quantities of water required for cooling purposes, these plants were to be sited alongside rivers, and thus we saw long stretches of our valleys affected. Not only do we have the eyesores of the large cooling towers and their billowing steam, we have forever to endure the emissions of ash far beyond the boundaries of the stations. We have also to realize the effect of the discharge of warm water from the cooling towers into the rivers – and the occasional accidental discharge of toxic waste. In fairness, it must be said that with vigilant control and good fortune, these have been few and far between. But when they have occurred, they have had a devastating effect on fish and wildlife. On at least one occasion, almost an entire flock of swans was poisoned and it took many years for the numbers to recover.

The huge pylons were erected in fields and towns, and they could in no way be anything but an eyesore. There was also the danger that the hooligan element would attempt to climb them, and some of course did and paid with their lives. After several years it was thought that the pylons close to dwellings were injurious to the health of inhabitants. The debate on this theory still carries on today. Whether or not there is a hazard, I have not been certain. What I have noticed, though, is that although we still have people demanding the supply of electricity, we do not appear to have as many pylons as we once had. I also notice that those which stood on the housing estate at Stapenhill vanished; maybe they get their supply in bottles, or am I just being sceptical?

For all the disadvantages, we now have a first-class electricity supply, and we must be thankful and realize that the times demand it.

A further bonus is that the heat discharged into the atmosphere and the warm water discharged into the river has caused a change in the local climate. We in Burton have not in recent years experienced such thick fogs or heavy snowfalls as we have in the past. I know that the general warming of the earth is taking place, but nevertheless, districts quite close to us still suffer more than we do. Those of you who travel only the short distances into Derbyshire and Leicestershire will notice that.

When electricity was first supplied to homes, our house at 11 Victoria Street was just about the first one to be done. I remember neighbours coming in to see its wonders. No mantles, no matches; just press a switch and you had a light. The two-way switch on the staircase was out of this world! The payment meter for this required a one-shilling coin, so now we had to make sure we had one when 'The bob went' and darkness fell upon us.

I know my parents had to pay for the installation, although I have no idea how much. If my memory serves me right, the price of the electricity which we used was reduced after we had used a quantity which was overpriced to offset installation costs.

The End of the 1990s

We are now about to enter a new millennium. I sometimes spend many sleepless hours, during which my mind wanders down many 'Memory Lanes'. As I lay awake in the early hours of this morning, I thought of Keith and John, with four of our grandsons, having a laugh together, and I realized that apart from John they were all taller than myself. Then, because it seemed only like yesterday that they were all little children who used to go upstairs with a television and a supply of sweets and other goodies, only to reappear for a replenishment of stock, it dawned on me that I must be older than I thought. Apart from a few creaking joints, I kid myself that I am doing wonders to belie my almost 80 years. The next realization is that my wife lying alongside me is in her late 70s and has had far more illness than I, and is now enjoying her happiest days. This then leads me on to a saying which my pal Len Williams quotes each week when we have our Sunday phone chat, 'We are the lucky ones, Jim. We are still here!'

As I lay and pondered on these thoughts, my mind went back to that small group of two generations, everyone happy, having not known the separations from their loved ones or undergone the same experiences as had we. THAT was the answer, that was what made it all worthwhile. If I live to be 100, I will always look back on that little group of happy people when I am feeling a bit low, and say to myself, 'Get up and have a laugh with them' – and I will, all by myself. Never again will I think that I have been hard done by. No more will I envy the youngsters their youth; that small group of two generations have given me the assurance that they will not waste it.

The part played by Dorothy in all this must not be forgotten. Not only was she seriously ill in hospital 12 miles from home for some months prior to the birth of David, experiencing air raids and in the knowledge that I was reported missing; when some had become convinced that I would not come home, Dorothy always kept up her spirits and made sure that both she and David would be there for me when I came home, which she always believed I would. We have always been deeply in love and have faced together whatever fate has thrown at us. Our long and happy marriage has been our reward. Of the two of us, Dorothy has had the more difficult passage, but I know that she would not thank me for expanding on that. Always aiming to spring a surprise on Dorothy, I knocked on the front door at 11.30pm on the night of 10 November 1945, having been unable to give warning that I was even in the country less than twenty-four hours previously. Dorothy was aroused from her sleep and came down with David in her arms, and thus we were introduced.

'Laugh and the world laughs with you,
Cry and you cry alone.'

'Make new friends and keep the old,
One is silver, the other is gold.'

Acknowledgements

Growing up I can remember many occasions being asked by all sorts of people "how's your Dad doing" and I would always reply "fine thanks" but not understanding why they would ask such a thing to a small boy?

It wasn't until later years that things became a little clearer and I realized that my father's experiences during WW2 had affected our family life and to some extent still do today. One of the reasons for our lack of knowledge was that it was a taboo subject in our home and there were very few conversations if any, regarding his experiences during those years. During his early days of recuperation my father was instructed by the RAF that under no circumstances must he discuss his treatment at the hands of the Japanese with anyone and likewise my mother was visited at home by the authorities and told not to raise the subject or ask him questions about his incarceration and how he was treated.

At home my father loved listening to his music on our Grundig Stereogram and had accumulated quite a collection of LP's (long playing vinyl records) After a while his enjoyment of music was interrupted when the stereogram started to malfunction causing the volume level to raise and lower without human intervention. It was the early 70's and it was time to buy a new music system. During this time the UK had become flooded with Japanese imports of all kinds including Cars, Motor Bikes and electrical goods. It was a Saturday morning when I watched my parents set off to town to buy a new stereo and I waited in anticipation as I wondered what make they would buy as no Japanese products of any kind were ever allowed to enter our home.

A couple of hours later my parents returned home with a new Aiwa stereo. It was the first Japanese object to cross our door step and it was to give our family, my father in particular, many hours of enjoyment for years to come. I wondered was this the first indication of acceptance of what had happened to him and his colleagues during those years.

Not long after that Jim Banton joined the FEPOW association – the Far East Prisoners Of War and became reunited with some of his old comrades. Jim attended many functions and meetings and particularly enjoyed the short breaks at Pontins Holiday Camp where the FEPOWs and their wives got together to reminisce and rekindle old friendships bonded together by a unique but horrifying part of their lives.

I would like to thank my sister Jacqueline and her husband John Stevenson for the assistance they have given me in helping to get our fathers memoirs published. My wife Jacquie has also been a great support during this project.

Several years ago I contacted a gentleman called Tim Love who has been a sound source of information and advice. Tim has visited Sumatra on several occasions over the years and in fact has travelled the entire length of what was the Sumatra Railway. During his visits he has taken many photographs and some of these are featured in this book. Tim has also been very active in trying to gain more recognition for the POWs of Sumatra.

Many years ago I remember and old friend of my father's came to visit us and stayed for Sunday tea. His name was Jack Brown who in civilian life was a Superintendent in a psychiatric hospital, he was also a POW. My father always maintained that this gentleman saved his life.

During their imprisonment it is well know that the POWs suffered a plethora of tropical diseases as well as starvation and brutal treatment from their captors both Japanese guards and later their Korean replacements. Many of the POWs succumbed to Melancholia which is a subtype of depression and they simply just gave up hope and passed away. It came to be that the prisoners could soon tell who would be the next to die by observing their behavior, and they would nod to one another as if to say 'he's next'! Sadly the POWs were more than often correct.

Thanks to Jack Brown's steadfast support and daily counselling sessions, disguised as friendly chit chat, my father avoided this cruel demise which enabled him to return home to his family and friends. Jack and my father remained friends for the rest of their lives and although I have to assume that Jack has since died I thank him on behalf of the Banton family and hope that some of his relatives get to read this.

Finally of course I thank both my parents for battling to survive their separate and numerous ordeals over the years. Without their steadfast determination to survive against the odds my sisters Jeanne and Jacqueline as well as myself would have not been born. They also had 9 grandchildren.

Together they enjoyed a long and happy retirement which they well deserved after all that they had endured during their lifetimes. Jim and